202 SCIENCE INVESTIGATIONS

exciting adventures
in earth, life,
and physical sciences

by Marjorie Frank
illustrated by Kathleen Bullock

Cover and illustrations by Kathleen Bullock
Edited by Sherri Y. Lewis

ISBN 0-86530-173-5

Contents

PHYSICAL SCIENCES

Welcome To
The Amazing World of Science

How is it possible for an egg to bounce and not break?
What could make raisins dance?
How can a slimy goop be both a liquid and a solid?

There are all kinds of unusual events such as these happening every-where in the natural world around you. They are things that happen for reasons, but often the reasons are pretty mysterious.

SCIENCE is the wonderful and often surprising experience of looking for the reasons. It is asking questions and discovering secrets about ordinary things like rocks and rain or about extraordinary things like comets and tornadoes.

SCIENCE is the exciting adventure of trying to solve mysteries. It is the way people apply their natural curiosity to learn and understand more about their world.

This book is full of investigations that will help you take a close look at some of the amazing things which go on around you. You'll use some scientific **processes** (see page 10) to find some answers to questions about **happenings** in your environment (see page 11).

Start by reading "How To Be A Good Scientist" (page 12) and the very important rules for "Safe Science" (page 13).

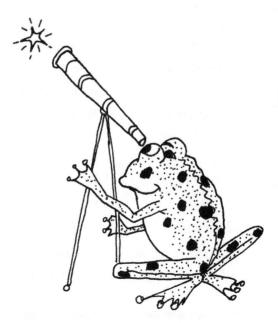

Then...
let your mind be open...
ask questions...
and have a great time...
performing and **discovering**
    some of the amazing wonders of
    science.

Science Is Doing . . .

Science is something that people do. These are the processes that scientists use to do science:

Observing	Using all the senses to gain information about objects and happenings (phenomena)
Measuring	Identifying length, width, mass, volume, or temperature of objects or happenings
Collecting	Gathering specimens and data
Identifying	Naming and describing objects and phenomena and their properties
Classifying	Sorting and grouping objects and events based on some common characteristics or relationships
Comparing & Contrasting	Seeing similarities and differences in objects, events, and relationships
Interpreting	Explaining the meaning of data collected
Sequencing	Putting objects and events in order according to size, importance, occurance, or other factors
Recognizing Relationships	Seeing connections and relationships between objects and events, including cause and effect relationships
Predicting	Using observations and previous discoveries to propose possible outcomes of future events
Inferring	Using collected data and observations to propose explanations of events that have occurred
Forming Hypotheses	Making guesses or assumptions to propose explanations/ results of a particular event or experiment
Experimenting	Setting up a controlled situation in order to test a hypothesis or a prediction
Controlling Variables	Recognizing and manipulating the factors that affect the outcome of events and experiments
Drawing Conclusions	Examining outcomes and making assumptions about what happened and why
Forming Models	Constructing a physical or mental representation of objects or events
Reporting & Recording	Communicating observations, data, and results — orally, visually, or in writing

. . . Science Is Finding Out

The processes for doing science help you learn about...

LIFE SCIENCES

Human bodies and their systems
Other animals
Plants
Animal families and groups
Plant and animal habitats
Life cycles
Life processes
Growth of plant and animals
The natural environment
Food chains
Ecosystems
Ecology and conservation
Health and fitness

PHYSICAL SCIENCES

States of matter
Properties of matter
Atoms and molecules
Physical changes in matter
Chemical changes in matter
Mixtures and solutions
Compounds and elements
Electricity
Magnetism
Forces
Energy sources
Heat
Sound
Light and color
Machines and work

EARTH & SPACE SCIENCES

The earth's resources
Ecology and conservation
Rocks and minerals
Changes in the earth
The history of the earth
Soil
Water
Air
Weather
The oceans and other waters
The seasons
The universe
The solar system
The night sky

How To Be A Good Scientist

Are you interested in finding answers to puzzling problems? Good! Then you're great scientist material.

Here are some hints for you to follow as you continue being a scientist.

BE CURIOUS
Keep your eyes wide open and watch for unusual things. Wonder about everything; don't take anything for granted. Constantly ask questions such as:
"What will happen?"
"Why is this happening?"
"What did I learn from this?"

BE ORGANIZED
Get all your materials together before you start an investigation. Read and follow directions carefully. Keep good records! Write down what you see and what you learn in a notebook. (In this book, many investigations have data sheets that go with them. Use these to keep records.)

BE WISE
Follow all the rules for safe science (see page 13), and take good care of your science equipment and supplies. You don't want to have a fun science adventure spoiled by an accident or broken equipment.

BE INVENTIVE
Don't be afraid to try different things, to ask more questions, to make guesses about what might happen, or to come up with a different way of checking out something. If something didn't work out or something is still puzzling you, try another experiment. Keep asking questions such as:
"What might happen if I tried this?"
"What more could I find out?"

BE PATIENT
Take plenty of time to perform your experiment or investigation. And if it doesn't work right, be willing to try again. Try to analyze why it didn't work, and keep trying.

ENJOY THE "DOING"!
Don't worry if you don't understand everything or find every answer. Even the most brilliant scientists don't understand everything. There are still lots of mysteries in the world of science. All the fun isn't in getting the answer, most is found in the process of looking for it!

Science Safety

Here are some simple rules to follow every time you perform science activities:

- ALWAYS get adult permission and help when you use fire or electricity.

- Tie back long hair and roll up baggy sleeves. Wear an old shirt or smock to protect clothes.

- Cover the work area with newspapers.

- Keep a bucket of cold water nearby at all times.

- Have a fire extinguisher and first-aid kit nearby.

- Before you start, read all the directions. Then follow them carefully.

- Always work cautiously and be alert. Be careful not to bump into others who are working.

- Take care with chemicals. Label each bottle and keep containers covered so they won't spill.

- Wear goggles if the experiment involves chipping rocks or any splashing.

- NEVER point the open end of a test tube toward yourself or others.

- NEVER put your face or eyes upclose to a chemical or mixture.

- NEVER taste, touch, or eat a substance unless you are told to by a reliable book or adult.

- Don't eat off utensils that have been used for science activities.

- Don't eat leaves or berries from plants you're studying.

- If you're working with animals, wear gloves, and touch the animals only if an adult tells you it's safe to do so.

- Use batteries and dry cells, not household current, as sources of electricity for your experiments.

- Remember that water and electricity are a deadly combination. Keep wet hands and water away from sources of electricity.

- When you're finished with an investigation, wash your hands and all utensils thoroughly, and clean up the work area completely.

Good Stuff To Collect For Science

Chemicals & Related Substances

alcohol
alum
baking soda
bleach
borax
charcoal
cornstarch
Epsom salts
flour
food coloring
fruit juices

ink
iodine
lemon juice
plaster of Paris
rock salt
sugar
vinegar
laundry detergent
  flakes
water
yeast

Cloth, Paper, & Such

adding machine tape
aluminum foil
balsa wood
cardboard boxes
cardboard scraps
cardboard tubes
cellophane
clear adhesive paper
cloth scraps
cotton balls
dowels
envelopes
paper: drawing paper
  construction paper
  tissue paper
  wax paper
paper bags
paper plates
paper towels
plastic bags
plastic wrap
tagboard
wood scraps

Containers

aluminum pans and
  trays
bottles, all sizes
coffee cans
cookie sheets
cottage cheese
  containers
drinking glasses
egg cartons
flowerpots
jars with lids

measuring cups
measuring spoons
milk cartons, all sizes
pails
petri dishes
pie pans
plastic jugs
pots & pans
tin cans, many sizes
trays
zip-up plastic bags

Equipment and Instruments

batteries
bells
bell wire
flashlight bulbs
candles
coat hangers
dry cells
eating utensils
electric fan
electric hot plate
eyedropper
filter paper

flashlight
glass lenses
glass pieces (smooth edges)
hammer
iron filings
litmus paper
magnets
magnifying glass
measuring sticks
measuring tape
mirrors

modeling clay
plastic tubing
prism
scale
scissors
sponges
stopwatch
teakettle
test tubes
thermometers
tweezers

Hardware and Other Items

balloons
bottle caps
buttons
broom handle
comb
corks
cotton swabs
crayons
fishing line
glue
marbles
matches

nails & screws
needles & pins
nuts & bolts
old inner tube
paint & brushes
paper clips
table tennis balls
rocks
rope
rubber cement
sand
sawdust

seeds & beans
small rubber balls
spools
steel wool
tape: scotch
          adhesive
          masking
thumbtacks
thread
toothpicks
yarn
straws
string

A Word To Teachers

Children are born scientists. They naturally probe, question, and test their environment. Your task is not to teach them to be curious but to encourage the inborn inquisitiveness, make the most of it, and share it with them. Your own curiosity and your enthusiasm are the best attributes you can bring to the science setting.

How To Use This Book:

This book is a collection of investigations that can serve as independent activities for an individual or small group, or as a basis for a whole group lesson. Each one may be used separately or incorporated into a broader science unit.

Each investigation gives a complete list of materials needed and complete directions for pursuing a question.

A "What's Happening?" section included on many pages provides a brief explanation for the events. This information may be for your use or may be shared with students. Think of this as only a beginning explanation, and work with students to find out more about each concept you investigate.

Data sheets also accompany many investigations. These direct students to collect and record data and provide a place for responses related to other processes.

The "processes" (page 10) are used in various combinations in each investigation. One of the greatest services you can offer to young scientists is practice in identifying and using these processes. Do this by planning to include several of them every time you have a science activity. Point them out as you use them. Frequently ask the kinds of questions that encourage students to use the processes:

> "What do you think will happen?"
> "When or where have you seen something like this before?"
> "What is happening?"
> "What do you see, smell, hear, feel, taste?"
> "What might happen if you tried this?"
> "How are these alike or different?"
> "What do you think this result means?"
> "How can we find out _____ ?"
> "What else could we try?"

Keep asking questions, keep wondering with your students, and have fun doing science with them!

Life Sciences

What Your Pulse Can Tell You

Pay attention to your pulse and learn some things about your heart.

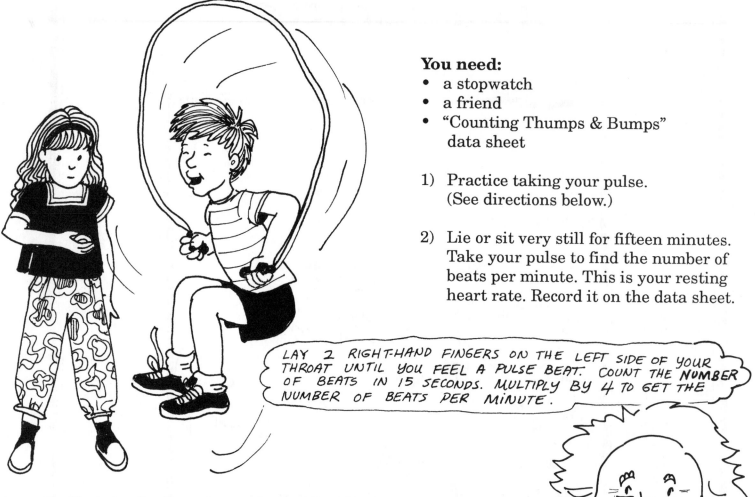

You need:
- a stopwatch
- a friend
- "Counting Thumps & Bumps" data sheet

1) Practice taking your pulse. (See directions below.)

2) Lie or sit very still for fifteen minutes. Take your pulse to find the number of beats per minute. This is your resting heart rate. Record it on the data sheet.

LAY 2 RIGHT-HAND FINGERS ON THE LEFT SIDE OF YOUR THROAT UNTIL YOU FEEL A PULSE BEAT. COUNT THE **NUMBER** OF BEATS IN 15 SECONDS. MULTIPLY BY 4 TO GET THE NUMBER OF BEATS PER MINUTE.

3) Exercise for five minutes by jogging slowly or jumping rope. Take your pulse. Record it.

4) Keep exercising. Record your pulse after ten and fifteen minutes.

5) After fifteen minutes of exercise, walk around very slowly for five minutes. Then take your pulse. This is called your recovery heart rate. Record it.

What's Happening?
Your pulse tells you how fast your heart is beating. The throb you feel is the blood rushing through the vessels with each heartbeat. During exercise your heart beats faster. When you stop, your heart rate slows down.

Investigation

Counting Thumps & Bumps

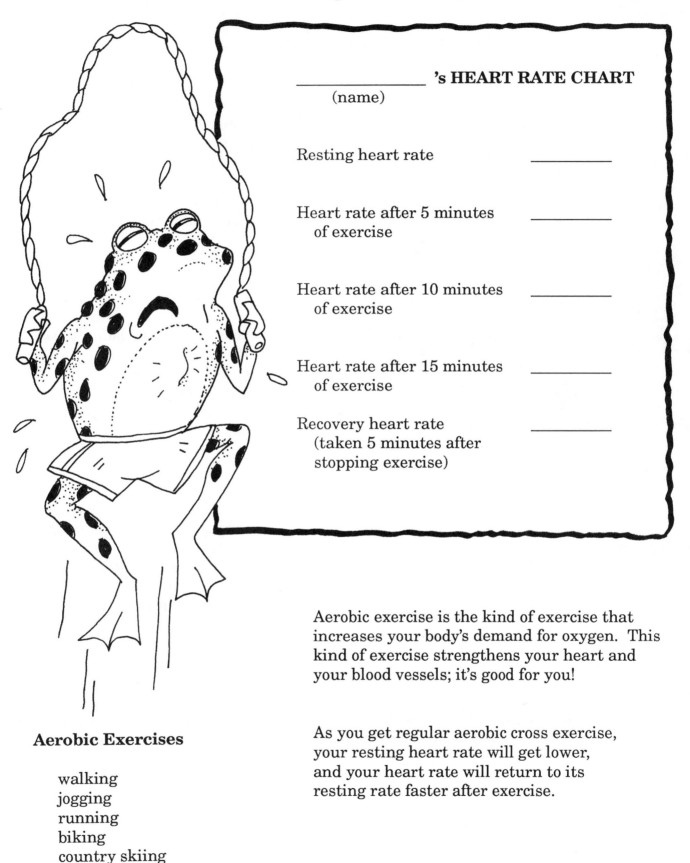

_____ 's HEART RATE CHART
(name)

Resting heart rate   _____

Heart rate after 5 minutes   _____
of exercise

Heart rate after 10 minutes   _____
of exercise

Heart rate after 15 minutes   _____
of exercise

Recovery heart rate   _____
(taken 5 minutes after
stopping exercise)

Aerobic exercise is the kind of exercise that increases your body's demand for oxygen. This kind of exercise strengthens your heart and your blood vessels; it's good for you!

As you get regular aerobic cross exercise, your resting heart rate will get lower, and your heart rate will return to its resting rate faster after exercise.

Aerobic Exercises

walking
jogging
running
biking
country skiing
swimming
jumping

Data Sheet

Listening In On Heart Sounds

Here are two simple stethescopes you can make to hear someone's heart beat.

You need:
- 2 feet of rubber tubing
- 2 small funnels
- scissors
- watch with a second hand
- sturdy paper cup
- a friend

1) Cut the bottom out of the cup. Put the largest end against a friend's chest just to the left of the center. Press your ear against the other end of the cup and listen. (Do not touch the cup with your hands.) How many beats do you hear in a minute?

OR

2) Insert a funnel into each end of the rubber tubing. Place one funnel against a friend's chest near the heart and the other end on your ear. Listen carefully. Count the heartbeats per minute.

What's Happening?
The paper cup and the funnels "magnify" the sounds of the heart making them loud enough for you to hear clearly. The heartbeat sounds are made by valves in the heart opening and closing.

How To See Your Pulse

Did you ever actually see your pulse? Here's a way to watch it with your own eyes.

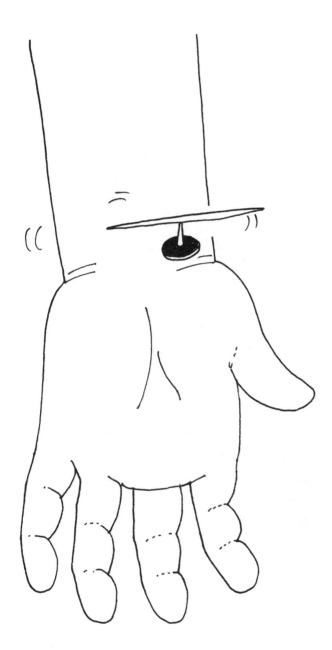

You need:
- thumbtacks
- toothpicks
- stopwatch or watch with a second hand

1) Push the sharp end of the thumbtack into the center of one toothpick.

2) Use two fingers to find the spot on your wrist where you can feel your pulse. Lay the head of the thumbtack on this spot.

3) Hold still and watch the toothpick. You should see it move with every heartbeat. Use the watch to help you find out how many times the toothpick moves in a minute.

What's Happening?

The blood rushes through your blood vessels with each contraction of your heart. This rushing causes your pulse. The force of the rush also causes your skin to move a little which makes the toothpick move.

Investigation

A Humerus Is Not Humorous

The humerus is sometimes called a funny bone. Do you know why? Do you know where it is? There are 206 bones hiding under your skin. Here's a way to find your humerus and lots of others!

You need:
- a partner
- shorts and a T-shirt to wear
- washable markers
- "Bone Map" data sheet

1) Look at the bone map. It will help you find some of the major bones in your body. Try to find each bone that's shown.

2) As you locate a bone, use a marker to label it right on your skin.

3) Talk with your partner about how each bone feels, and compare the sizes of the different bones. Did you find your two funny bones?

What makes the humerus "funny"? A nerve passes near to the inside of the knob at the end of the humerus. When you bang that spot, the nerve presses against the bone and causes a sharp tingling feeling. There's really nothing funny about it, is there?

Bone Map

Find these bones. Label each one on your body. Color each one after you've found it.

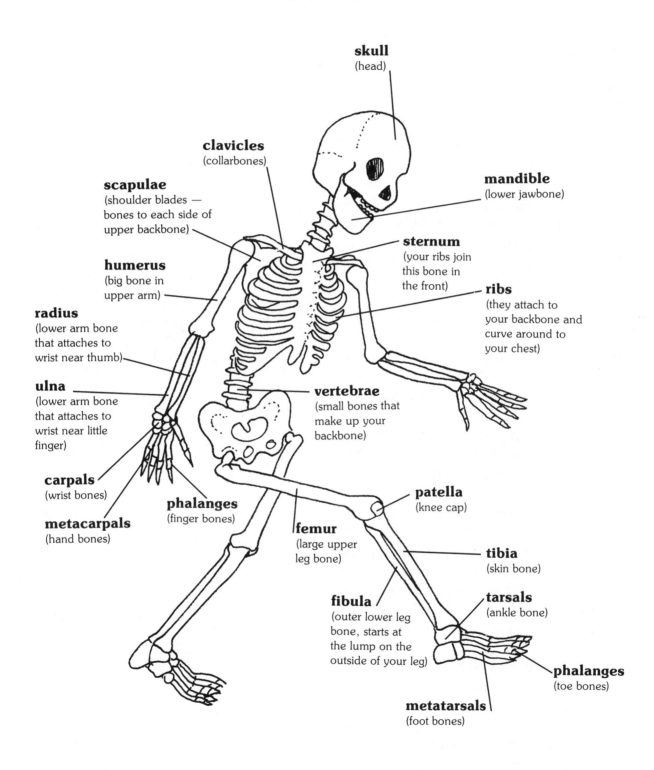

skull
(head)

clavicles
(collarbones)

scapulae
(shoulder blades —
bones to each side of
upper backbone)

mandible
(lower jawbone)

humerus
(big bone in
upper arm)

sternum
(your ribs join
this bone in
the front)

radius
(lower arm bone
that attaches to
wrist near thumb)

ribs
(they attach to
your backbone and
curve around to
your chest)

ulna
(lower arm bone
that attaches to
wrist near little
finger)

vertebrae
(small bones that
make up your
backbone)

carpals
(wrist bones)

patella
(knee cap)

metacarpals
(hand bones)

phalanges
(finger bones)

femur
(large upper
leg bone)

tibia
(skin bone)

fibula
(outer lower leg
bone, starts at
the lump on the
outside of your leg)

tarsals
(ankle bone)

phalanges
(toe bones)

metatarsals
(foot bones)

Data Sheet

Make Yourself A Second Set of Teeth

Get a close-up look at your teeth without even taking them out of your mouth.

You need:
- modeling clay
- lightweight cardboard
- toothpicks
- toothbrush
- plaster of Paris
- large paper cup
- "Which Teeth Are Which" data sheet
- foil
- tape
- water
- old spoon
- 8 hours
- newspapers

1) Shape the clay into a "cookie" about 3/4" thick that will fit inside your mouth.

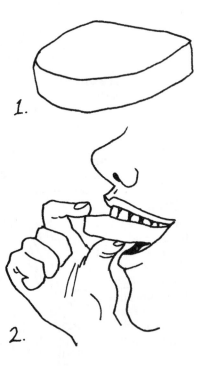

1.

2) Bite into it with your top teeth and press the clay around your teeth. Make sure you push it up to your gums on all sides. Then carefully pull the mold away from your teeth.

3) Repeat this for your bottom teeth.

4) Make a cardboard collar about 2 inches tall for each mold. Tape them to hold snugly to the molds. Set them on foil.

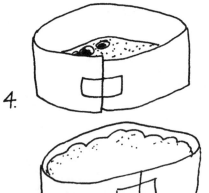

2.

5) Fill the paper cup about half full of dry plaster of Paris. Add enough water to make a thick, creamy liquid.

6) Use toothpicks and toothbrush to dab small amounts of plaster down into all the tiny spaces made by your teeth. Tap the mold to make sure the plaster of Paris sets in. Then pour in the plaster of Paris to fill the molds. Tap the molds on the table to get rid of air bubbles.

4.

7) After these sit for eight hours, tear off the collars and gently pull the clay away from your teeth.

6.

8) Look at the data sheet and locate each kind of tooth on your new set of teeth.

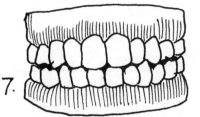

7.

Which Teeth Are Which?

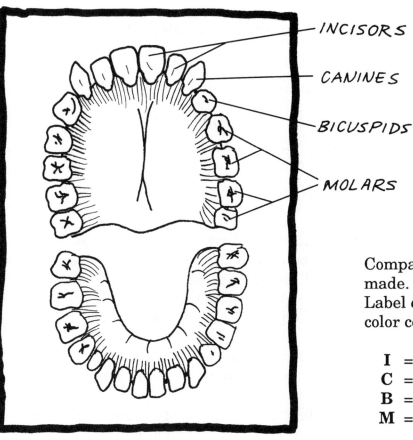

INCISORS

CANINES

BICUSPIDS

MOLARS

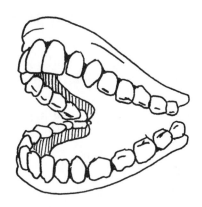

Compare this to the new set of teeth you've made.

Label each tooth on your cast of teeth or color code them with markers.

I = Incisor (or color these blue)
C = Canine (or color these red)
B = Bicuspid (or color these green)
M = Molars (or color these purple)

INCISORS
4 on top, 4 on bottom
These 8 front teeth work together like scissors when you bite.

BICUSPIDS
4 flat teeth, 1 to the outside of each canine
These teeth have two points on them. They are good food-crunchers.

CANINES
4 pointed sharp teeth, 1 to the outside of each incisor
These are good for tearing meat. Dogs have very large ones.

MOLARS
4 on each side, top and bottom
These larger teeth in the back are great for grinding and mashing food into small bits.

Data Sheet

The Digestion Question

What happens to your lunch? Here's a way to keep track of it after it's gone!

You need:
- peanut butter & jelly sandwich
- clock
- crayons
- "Down The Tube" data sheet

1) The data sheet shows a diagram of the tube your food travels through after you eat it. Look at the descriptions of the parts of the food tube, and notice the places to record the time when your lunch will be in each part.

2) Get your clock ready. Write down the starting time, then immediately eat the sandwich.

3) Pay attention to the time the sandwich spends in your mouth. When you're done swallowing the last bite, record the time.

4) Keep following the sandwich through the digestive system. Since you can't actually see or feel when it enters or leaves each part of the tube, you'll have to estimate the time it spends there. The data sheet information will help you.

5) Over the next day or two, remember to be thinking at all times where your sandwich might be.

Investigation

Down The Tube

Record the approximate time the sandwich leaves each section of the tube.

Color that section when you think the sandwich has passed through it.

Times

_____ **STARTING TIME**

_____ **MOUTH**
Teeth, tongue, and saliva all begin to work on food to break it into small pieces.

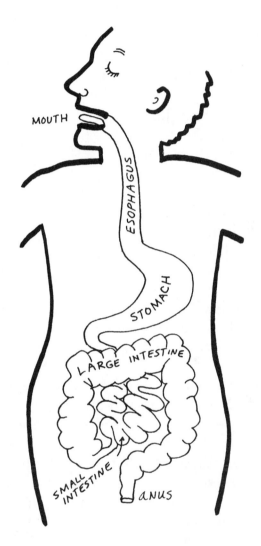

_____ **GULLET**
(esophagus)
This muscular tube squeezes and pushes food down into the stomach in <u>less than ten seconds per mouthful</u>.

_____ **STOMACH**
A stretchy, strong balloon-shaped part of the tube. It closes shut and starts to work squeezing, mashing, and mixing food with strong fluids, all of which help to break it up into tiny pieces. The food ends up as a mushy soup. <u>This takes up to four hours</u>.

_____ **SMALL INTESTINE**
A 20 foot long curled-up tube. Here digestive juices pour in from the liver, pancreas, and gallbladder to mix with food as it is moved along by squeezing muscles. Most of the food gets absorbed through the walls of the small intestine right into the blood which carries it around the body to be used or stored away. <u>Plan about eight hours for food</u> to get through this maze!

_____ **LARGE INTESTINE**
In the last 4 to 5 feet of the tube, the parts of our food that can't be used are collected. Water is removed from it to be recycled, and the remaining solids are disposed through the opening which is called the **anus**. <u>Food may take a day or two to move through the large intestine</u>.

Data Sheet

Whose Fingerprints?

All human beings belong to the same species, and we're all alike in many ways. But every one of us has different fingerprints!

You need:
- inked stamp pad
- 3" x 5" blank index cards
- pens
- tall drinking glass
- typing paper
- masking tape
- soap
- water
- paper towels
- magnifying glass
- lots of friends
- "The Great Fingerprint Mystery" data sheet

SUDDENLY, EVERYONE'S A DETECTIVE!

1) Use index cards to make two sets of fingerprint cards for each person. Use separate cards for each hand. (See page 29.)

2) Practice making fingerprints:
   - Wash and dry your hands well.
   - Ink your thumb by rolling it lightly from one edge to the other on the ink pad.
   - Press it firmly onto a piece of white paper in the same way — rolling it from one side to the other.
   - Practice making prints until you can get clear, unsmeared prints that show the lines.

3) Help each other make prints of all ten fingers carefully on the cards. Do one fingerprint at a time.

4) Look at the types of prints on the next page. Label each of your prints with "A," "L," or "W."

5) Now that you have everyone's prints on file, do some detective work. Set up and solve the mystery on the data sheet.

Investigation

The Great Fingerprint Mystery

Wrap white typing paper around a drinking glass. Tape it securely.

Choose five people to be detectives. Send them out of the room. Everyone else is a suspect. Choose one to be the culprit who commits a "crime" and leaves fingerprints on the glass. (This person inks fingers and holds the glass with both hands to leave clear prints.) Then, the detectives return. They can solve the mystery by comparing the prints on the glass to the fingerprint cards.

FINGERPRINT CARD

LEFT HAND:

1. Thumb   2. Fore finger   3. Index   4. Ring   5. Pinkie

RIGHT HAND:

1. Thumb   2. Fore finger   3. Index   4. Ring   5. Pinkie

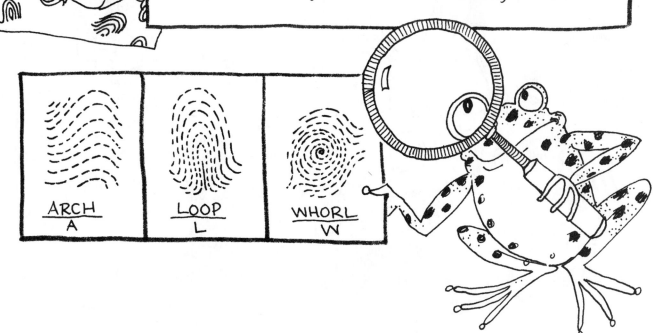

ARCH
A

LOOP
L

WHORL
W

The War Against Germs

Germs can make you sick even though they're often too tiny to see. But your body is smart. It knows how to defend you against most germs. Get some friends together to play this game of waging war against germs.

You need:
- 20-30 people
- lots of space
- labels or costumes for players

1) Choose players for the roles:

1	ear
1	cut on skin
1	mouth
1	nose
2	eyes
10-15	skin
8-10	white blood cells
5-10	germs

2) Make costumes or labels for all characters.

3) Read the information on the next page to learn how the body defends itself against germs.

4) Set up the game:

"Skin" players join hands to form as large a circle as possible.

"Ear," "Eyes," "Cut," "Mouth," and "Nose" take different places as part of the circle.

"Blood Cells" start inside the circle.

"Germs" start outside the circle.

5) Start the game:

- The germs try to get into the body by breaking through it. The most susceptible places of course are the ears, eyes, nose, mouth, and cut.

- The people in the circle must stay in place and try to keep germs out.

- When a germ does enter the body, the white blood cells try to surround it and carry it out of the circle.

HOW YOUR BODY DEFENDS ITSELF AGAINST GERMS

SKIN
Forms a very strong wall that keeps out germs. Sweat from the pores helps kill germs.

EYES
Tears wash away dirt and kill germs.

NOSE
Hairs and mucus filter out dirt and germs.

MOUTH
Saliva washes germs to the stomach where the strong juices kill them.

EARS
Wax traps dirt and germs.

CUTS
Inside a cut, a special glue-like substance in your blood forms a kind of fence (scab) to keep out germs.

WHITE BLOOD CELLS
These destroy the germs that get inside your body.

Investigation

How Hot Is Hot?

Play this trick on your hands and they won't be able to tell hot from cold.

You need:
- 1 bowl 1/2 full of hot water
- 1 bowl 1/2 full of room temperature water
- 1 bowl 1/2 full of cold water
- timer

1) Set the timer for three minutes.

2) Put your left hand in the hot water and your right hand in the cold water.

3) When the timer rings, take both hands out and shake them off. Put both hands immediately into the room temperature water. How does this feel to the left hand...hot or cold? How does this feel to the right hand...hot or cold?

What's Happening?
The room temperature water feels different to both hands because the messages sent from the hands' sensory receptors to the brain are confused. Your right hand adapted to the cold water, so it senses the room temperature water as hot. The left hand adapted to the hot water, so it senses the room temperature water as cold.

Investigation

Hands On Ice

Pick up a penny? Easy as pie...right?
Don't be so sure!

You need:
- timer
- a friend
- small bag of ice
- jacket with a zipper
- 5 pennies
- 5 straight pins

1) Put the jacket on without zipping it.

2) Spread the pennies and pins on a table or the floor.

3) Hold the bag of ice in your right hand for two minutes.

4) Pick up the pennies and pins with that hand. What happens?

5) Hold the bag of ice in your other hand for two minutes. Ask a friend to pinch an inch of skin on the back of both hands. Which one hurts more?

6) Warm your hands for a bit. Then hold the bag of ice with both hands for two minutes.

7) Try to zip the jacket.

What's Happening?
Cold dulls the sense of feeling in the nerve endings in your hands. This makes it difficult for you to pick up the pennies and pins, feel the pinch, or zip the jacket.

This is hard to do!

Investigation

Mystery Boxes

Which of your five senses is needed to solve each mystery?

You need:
- a friend or group of classmates
- blindfold
- 20 small boxes with lids
- sharp object for poking holes
  these objects or others like them:

- onion slice
- dry Cheerios₀
- baby rattle
- salt
- pepper
- coffee beans
- sandpaper
- sugar
- worm
- hard candy
- strip of potato
- "What's The Sense?"
  data sheet

- orange slice
- cinnamon stick
- glob of gelatin
  (in plastic bag)
- corn flakes
- ticking clock
- marbles
- balloon partly
  filled with air
- carrot strip
- cotton ball
- dry beans
- dry rice

Sniff
Sniff

1) Poke tiny holes in each box top not big enough to see through. Then number each box.

2) Put on the blindfold while your friend places an object in each box.

3) Now pick up one box at a time. Use your ears and nose to try to tell what is in it. If you need to, open the box and touch or taste it. You may take off the blindfold and look at it, too.

4) For each box, your friend should mark the data sheet chart with a "1" to show which sense was most important in your identification. Also check other senses that helped.

5) Now give your friend a chance to solve the mysteries.

Investigation

What's The Sense?

Peekaboo!

Put a "1" by the main sense.
Put a "✓" by others that helped.

BOX #	OBJECT	SMELL	TASTE	SIGHT	HEARING	TOUCH

Data Sheet

Tongue Travels

Have you ever seen a tongue map? You just might need one to help you learn your way around your tongue because different parts are for tasting different tastes.

You'll need:
- small cups
- toothpicks
- lemon juice
- "Getting To Know Your Tongue" data sheet
- spoons
- salty water
- sweet juice
- strong black tea
- facial tissues

1) Dry your tongue with a tissue. Hold your nose. Use a toothpick to drip a drop of salty water on the front of your tongue. Try a drop on the side, middle, and back drying your tongue before each test.

    Where is the saltiness strongest? Record the results of each taste test on your data sheet.

2) Repeat the taste test with drops of something sweet (juice), something bitter (tea), and something sour (lemon juice).

3) Look carefully at your chart. Does it help learn which areas of the tongue identify different tastes? Use the information to label the tongue map with the different tastes.

Investigation

Getting To Know Your Tongue

Type of Taste	Description of Tastes on Tongue			
	Front	Sides	Center	Back
Salty Salty Water				
Sweet Juice or Punch				
Sour Lemon Juice				
Bitter Strong Black Tea				

A MAP OF YOUR TONGUE

Label the tongue map to show which sections taste the different tastes, "SWEET," "SOUR," "BITTER," "SALTY."

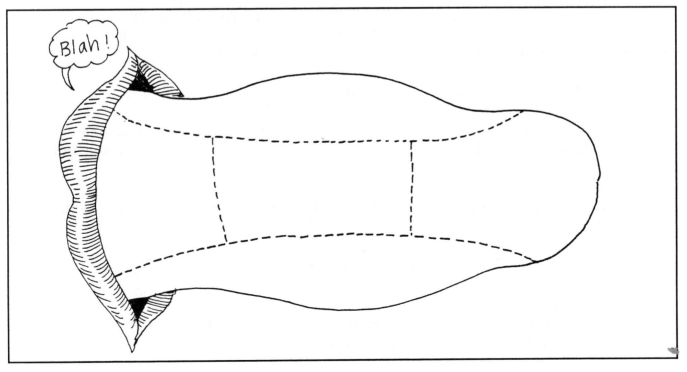

37

Data Sheet

What Your Nose Knows That Your Tongue Doesn't

Just how good is your taster? Hold your nose and try to identify some foods by taste alone.

You need:
- a friend
- blindfold
- toothpicks
- "Taste Testing" data sheet

- peeled cubes of vegetables and fruits listed (page 39)
- cups with small amounts of other foods listed

1) Blindfold yourself well, and hold your nose.

2) Have your friend use a toothpick to place one food at a time on the same spot on your tongue. Your friend should record your guess in the "Guess #1" column on the data sheet.

3) Now repeat the experiment without holding your nose. Record guesses in the "Guess #2" column.

4) Give your friend a chance to guess the foods, too.

What's Happening?
What we think of as taste is really a combination of smell and taste. When you hold your nose, you miss part of the familiar taste of each food.

Investigation

38

Taste Testing

Guess #1 holding nose	Guess #2 not holding nose	Food
		APPLE
		POTATO
		CELERY
		CARROT
		ONION
		PEACH
		PEAR
		ORANGE
		CHEESE
		TURNIP
		SALT
		SUGAR
		PEANUT BUTTER
		COLA
		CLEAR SOFT DRINK
		KETCHUP
		MUSTARD
		ORANGE JUICE
		LEMON JUICE

Data Sheet

Body Tricks

How touchy are you? Try these feeling tests and find out!

This one feels a little tricky...

GROAK

You need:
- a friend
- tweezers
- blindfold
  several objects such as:
- baseball cap
- apple
- walnut
- key
- "I've Got A Feeling" data sheet
- orange
- golf ball
- washcloth
- eraser
- spoon
- fork

1) Take your shoes off and have your friend blindfold you.

2) Touch each object with your feet one at a time, and try to tell what the object is. Your friend should mark each correct guess on the data sheet.

3) Now touch each object with your hands and guess again.

4) Next, blindfold your friend. Touch his skin gently with both prongs of the tweezers in each of the places listed on the data sheet. For each one your friend should tell you how many points can be felt, then you record it.

What's Happening?
Some parts of the body feel things better than others. There are sensitive nerve endings all over your skin, but some places have more than others and can feel things better. The middle of the back and the feet have fewer. The tongue and fingertips have many.

Investigation

I've Got A Feeling

Write down the names of the objects you'll try to pick up.

Put a check next to each one named correctly when touched with feet.

Do the same for each object named correctly when touched with hands.

Below, write the number of points felt in each spot during the tweezers' test.

OBJECT NAME	FEET	HANDS
1.		
2.		
3.		
4.		
5.		
6.		
7.		
8.		
9.		
10.		

TWEEZERS' TOUCH

	NUMBER OF POINTS FELT
ARM	
SHOULDER	
MIDDLE OF BACK	
KNEE	
FINGERTIP	
BACK OF HAND	
PALM OF HAND	
TONGUE	
SOLE OF FOOT	

Data Sheet

Reflex Hunt

A reflex is something your body does without your telling it to, like blinking or sneezing. Snoop around and see how many reflexes you can catch in action.

I just hate being cold and wet! Don't you?

You need:
- a whole day (or more)
- lots of people to spy on
- "Name That Reflex" data sheet

1) Look at the data sheet and read the descriptions of different reflexes.

2) Try to name each reflex. All are things you've done many times.

3) Watch people carefully for the next few days. Try to catch someone showing or "doing" a reflex. When you see one, write down the name of the person who showed it.

What's Happening?

All reflexes work through the lower part of the nervous system without going through the brain. The sensors sense something and send messages to the places in the nervous system which control the particular body movement. The message goes only from the sensors to the spinal cord and back to the muscles. Because they don't have to go all the way to the brain, reflexes are very fast. This happens automatically without your having to think about it!

Investigation

42

Name That Reflex

Achoooo

Dirt or dust gets in someone's nose. The nerves in the nose send a message to the spinal cord that the dirt is not supposed to be there. The spinal cord nerves tell the diaphragm to push a strong blast of air out of the lungs to get rid of the dirt.	This reflex is called _____ Person _____
Someone gets out of the shower, all wet. Nerves in the skin feel the cold air and send that message to the spinal cord, which tells muscles all over the body to start tightening and loosening in order to warm the cold body.	This reflex is called _____ Person _____
Nerves that control the diaphragm have been irritated by something and cause a spasm of the diaphragm which causes a person to gulp air. Just at that time, the space at the back of the throat near the vocal cords bangs shut with a loud sound.	This reflex is called _____ Person _____
The lungs are getting low on oxygen. Nerves carry this message to the spinal cord. The spinal cord tells the mouth to open wide and take a deep breath of air to give extra oxygen to the lungs.	This reflex is called _____ Person _____
Something tickles or scratches the throat. The scratching message is carried by nerves to the respiratory center at the top of the spinal cord. The spinal cord sends messages to muscles which cause a gulp of air, and other muscles close off part of the throat. Trapped air builds up pressure in the lungs, and when it rushes out to clear the throat, it makes a loud noise.	This reflex is called _____ Person _____
When bright light rushes into the eyes, nerves from the eyes take the message to the spinal cord that there's too much light. A message goes to a muscle in each eye (the iris) telling it to make the hole (pupil) smaller and to let in less light.	This reflex is called _____ Person _____

Data Sheet

Why You Don't Look Like Me

Have you ever wondered why you can't curl your tongue like your friend can? Or why your neighbor has freckles and you don't? Tiny little things called genes have a lot to do with what makes you YOU.

Help! I've got ears like my uncle Fred!

At least he's got ears!

You need:
- a week to do some research
- a mirror
- "Genes Run In Families" data sheet

1) Look in the mirror at the shape of your nose. Draw it in the "nose" space on the data sheet.

2) Compare it to the noses of some classmates.

3) Look for a family member whose nose has a similar shape. If you find one, write that person's name on the data sheet.

4) Do the same with other characteristics (traits) listed on the data sheet.

What's Happening?
Inside the nucleus (control center) of every cell in your body are twenty-three pairs of tiny threads called chromosomes. Along each thread are thousands of tiny bits called genes. Every gene contains a chemical formula, sort of a blueprint, for making some characteristic (called a trait) in you. Except for identical twins, every person has a different combination of traits. Traits are passed along to you by your parents and their parents.

Investigation

Genes Run In Families

Here are some traits decided by your genes. Draw or write each of yours on the chart.

For each one, try to find a relative who shares this trait.

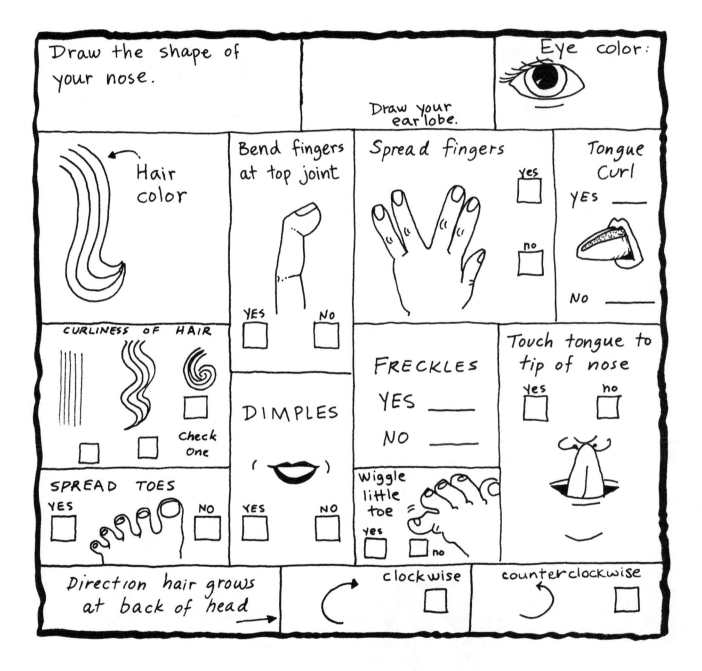

Data Sheet

Microinvestigation

You'll have to get on your belly to do this close-up examination of living things.

You need:
- magnifying glass
- 4 tongue depressors
- piece of string 4 meters long
- spoon
- plastic zip-up bag
- 1/2 hour to spend outdoors
- "It's A Small World" data sheet

1) Choose an outdoor spot to investigate. It can be a lawn, playground, field, dirt patch, a forest, or beside a pond.

2) Stake out an area for study by laying down the string to form a square. Use the tongue depressors for stakes at the four corners.

3) Get down on your belly and start looking very closely at all the stuff in your square. Try to keep your face 1 foot from the ground or closer.

4) Watch closely. Touch things gently. Notice how they feel. Is anything moving?

5) Use the spoon to collect some soil, grass, or other interesting specimens from your square.

6) Look at tiny things through the magnifying glass.

7) Use your data sheet to draw or write about some of the things you notice. Share your observations and your samples with a friend.

Investigation

46

It's A Small World

Some small things I saw:

Draw your favorite thing.

Tell about a sound you noticed.

Draw something that moved.

Describe something you touched.
Tell how it felt.

What surprised you?

What did you collect in your bag?

Draw one item you collected.

Data Sheet

Outdoor Scavenger Hunt

Get a bunch of friends or classmates together, and have a good time tracking outdoor treasures.

Don't worry, little caterpillar, I'll let you go again.

You need:
- some friends

these items for each player or team:
- spoon
- 3 small paper cups
- 3 small plastic zip-up bags
- 3 large plastic zip-up bags
- "I Found It!" data sheet

1) Look at the list of outdoor objects on the data sheet. Your goal for this scavenger hunt is to find as many of these as you can.

2) Decide with the other players if you will each hunt alone or if you will form teams. Also, agree on times to start and end the hunt.

3) As you find an object, put it in a bag or cup, and check it off on your data sheet.

4) When the hunt is over, see who has found the most objects on the list.

5) Return any living objects to the outdoors. Use some of the others to create a collage, picture, or creature.

Investigation

I Found It!

Find as many of these as you can!

something fuzzy

thistle or thorn

something sticky

needle from an evergreen

flower

live leaf

dead leaf

piece of litter

tree branch

acorn

leaf with spores

seedpod

cocoon

clover

rock showing erosion

mud

bug

egg (or part of one)

something beautiful

seed

feather

ant

bud

something that makes
  a noise

piece of fungus

pinecone

water sample

2 twigs

weed

part of a bird's nest

sandy soil

small pebble

49

Data Sheet

Fabulous Fruit Fly Farms

If you can catch some fruit flies in late summer, you'll have what you need to keep a fruit fly farm running for a long time.

You need:
- 3 widemouth jars with lids
- cloth and rubber bands
- overripe banana
- paper towels
- magnifying glass
- Fruit Fly Treat (see recipe)
- dry yeast
- tweezers
- water
- microscope (optional)

Investigation

1) Catch the fruit flies: Put a spoon full of the banana in a jar. Leave the lid off and fruit flies will gather. When you have six to eight flies, put the lid on and place the jar in the refrigerator.

2) Get the farmhouse ready: Make the Fruit Fly Treat and put about 1 inch of it in the bottom of a jar. Shake yeast on top of it. Crumple up a paper towel and place it in the jar. Sprinkle water on it.

3) Transfer the flies: The fruit flies can't fly when they're cold, so you can shake them into the farmhouse. Then use a rubberband to hold a piece of cloth over the top of the jar.

4) Watch the farm: Watch the flies as they eat, lay eggs, and hatch new flies. Count them every day.

How many days does it take to hatch new fruit flies?

Keep track of how many new ones are born.

You can take the fruit flies out of the jar any time to examine them. Just chill them so they stay calm, and handle them carefully with tweezers.

ENLARGED PICTURE OF A FRUIT FLY

If possible, look at them under a microscope and draw one here.

Spying on Spiders

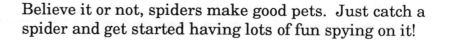

Believe it or not, spiders make good pets. Just catch a spider and get started having lots of fun spying on it!

You need:
- jar with lid
- magnifying glass
- live flies or mealworms
- small amount of dirt
- piece of a sponge
- water
- drinking glass
- piece of cardboard

1) Get the spider hotel ready. Place some dirt in the bottom of the jar. Add a twig and the sponge dampened with water. Punch tiny air holes in the lid. (Only one spider to a hotel, please!)

2) Catch a spider. Look in corners and near ceilings. When you see one, put the drinking glass over it, and slide the cardboard over the glass to trap the spider. Transfer it to the spider hotel.

3) Take good care of the spider. Keep the sponge damp with water and provide live flies or mealworms for food.

We should have made reservations!

4) Now you're ready to do some spider watching. Spend at least ten minutes at a time observing your new pet. Do this over a period of many days and weeks. Below are some questions and ideas to help with your spider watch.

Things to watch for:
How does it move?
How does it eat?
Does it molt (shed its skin)?
Can you find its eyes?
How does it clean itself?
Can you tell if it is male or female?
Does it lay eggs?
How do the eggs look?

Things to do:
Watch the spider making a web.
Draw the web and describe it.
Draw the spider.
Give it a name.
Keep a spider diary, writing what you observe each day.
Write a poem or story about your spider.
Go to the library and find a book about spiders. Try to find out what kind yours is, and learn as much as you can about spiders.

Investigation

Spend Some Time With A Worm

Bring some worms into your home or classroom. You'll be surprised how much fun they are to catch and watch and race.

You need:
- soil and peat moss
- wooden box or glass terrarium
- magnifying glass
- shovel
- fresh grass
- paper towels
- vegetable scraps and peels
- water
- piece of glass with smooth edges
- drawing paper
- ruler

1) Make a home for worms: Get a good-sized wooden box or glass terrarium. Mix soil and peat moss together in the box and add some water until it is damp but not soggy.

2) Catch some worms: Find a damp spot in a garden or lawn. Dig up a shovel-full of dirt. It will probably have worms in it. Or, scatter bits of bread and cheese and cornmeal over a damp spot, cover it with a heavy cloth, and wait until worms come to the surface. Put the worms in the box.

3) Feed the worms: Every few days sprinkle vegetable peels and scraps, fresh grass, or fresh leaves over the top of the dirt.

4) Watch them: Place a worm on a damp paper towel and watch it for a while. Examine it carefully under a magnifying glass. On the next page you'll find some ideas of things to look for and do with the worm.

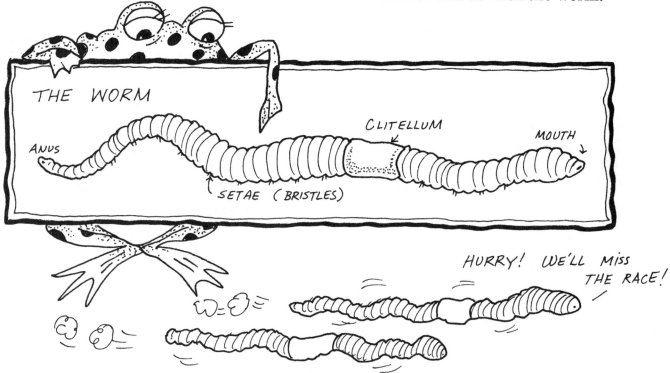

THE WORM

ANUS

SETAE (BRISTLES)

CLITELLUM

MOUTH

HURRY! WE'LL MISS THE RACE!

Draw your worm here.

Does it have eyes?

Does it have a mouth?

Does it have legs?

Place the worm on a damp paper towel and watch how it moves. Notice the pairs of small bristles on each segment of the worm. Touch the bristles.

Put the worm on a piece of paper and listen to it move.

Find the head, the darker end.

Find the back end which is flatter.

Find the clitellum, the band near the front end.

Turn the worm upside down and watch how it turns back over.

Place the worm on the glass piece. Hold it up to the light and look through the bottom. Can you see the blood vessels? Can you see the heart beating?

5) Have a worm race: Find an area of bare, hard ground outside. Use a stick to draw a 3 foot wide circle. Put several worms in the center of the circle. The winner is the worm that crosses the edge of the circle first.

ON YOUR MARK... GET SET... GO!

Investigation

55

Bug Watch

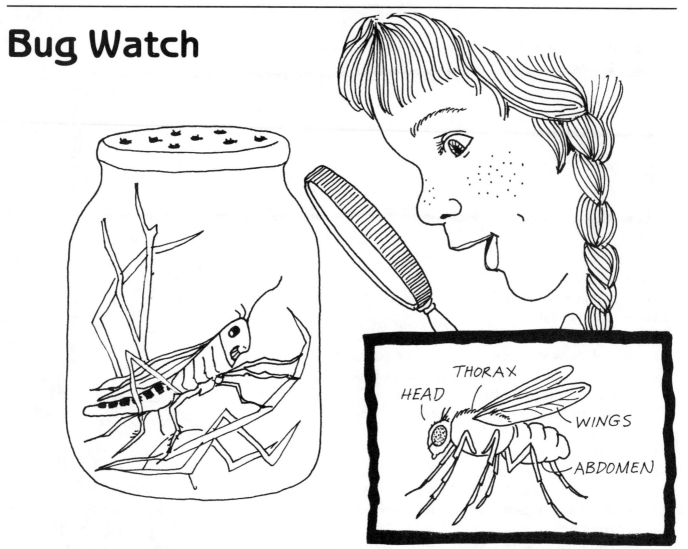

Catch a grasshopper and some other crawly creatures and learn why some bugs are insects and some are not.

You need:
- a jar with a lid that has small holes poked in it
- twigs and grass
- water
- grasshopper

- 1 or 2 ants
- at least 5 other bugs
- magnifying glass
- "Insect Check" data sheet

1) Catch a grasshopper and put it in the jar. Add some grass and twigs, and sprinkle in some water.

2) Use your magnifying glass to examine the grasshopper upclose. Decide if the grasshopper is an insect. Use the insect checklist on the data sheet to help you figure it out.

3) Draw the grasshopper on your sheet and check "yes" or "no" for your answer.

4) Let the grasshopper go free. Then repeat steps one through three with ants and at least four more bugs.

What's Happening?
All insects have the four characteristics shown on the next page. Any bugs without all these are not insects.

Investigation

Insect Check

Grasshopper

yes ___
no ___

Ant

yes ___
no ___

Bug 3

yes ___
no ___

Bug 4

yes ___
no ___

Bug 5

yes ___
no ___

Bug 6

yes ___
no ___

INSECT CHECKLIST

___ 6 Legs

___ 3 Separate body parts

___ 3 Pairs of legs

___ 1 Pair of antennae

___ Hard shell-like covering or hard outer body

Data Sheet

Footprints

Look for animal tracks in the woods or in your own backyard, and bring them home to keep.

You need:
- plaster of Paris
- water
- empty milk cartons (tops cut off)
- plastic cup
- petroleum jelly
- cardboard
- scissors
- old spoon
- old kitchen knife
- paper towels
- masking tape
- old toothbrush

1) Pack your supplies, go outside, and look for a track you'd like to keep.

2) When you find one, clean it off by gently removing any leaves or twigs.

3) Cut a cardboard strip about 2 inches wide. Bend it into a collar that will surround the track and tape it securely shut.

4) Grease the collar with petroleum jelly and push it into the ground to surround the track.

5) Mix plaster of Paris in a milk carton. Start with a cup of water and stir in the plaster of Paris gradually. Add it until you have a thick, creamy, pudding-like mixture.

6) Pour the plaster of Paris into the track up to the edge of the collar. Tap it to release air bubbles, and smooth off the top with a knife.

7) In a half hour it should be firm enough to remove from the ground and peel off the collar. This is the negative mold.

WOW! LOOK AT THESE NEAT FOOT- PRINTS!

Investigation

58

8) If you wish, you can now make a positive print. When the negative mold is very dry, clean it well and grease it with a thin layer of petroleum jelly. Use the toothbrush to get it into all the small spaces and places.

9) Make another collar to fit this mold. Grease the inside with petroleum jelly and tape it securely around the mold.

10) Make more plaster of Paris to pour into the mold. Tap it to release air bubbles, and smooth the top with a knife.

11) Wait two hours. Then carefully remove the collar and gently pull apart the positive and negative molds.

12) Back at home or school, clean the petroleum jelly off the molds with warm soapy water. These molds can be varnished or painted.

13) Use an encyclopedia or book about animal tracks to identify the footprint.

CAUTION: Do not wash any plaster of Paris down your sink!

Pickle Jar Germination

Germination is the beginning of the growth of a seed. Get a close-up look at this process by growing seeds without dirt in a pickle jar. But, first you have to eat the pickles!

BEANS, LENTILS, PEAS, ALFALFA, VEGETABLES,... FLOWERS.....

You need:
- pickle jar with a top
- seeds (beans, lentils, peas, alfalfa, flower, vegetable)
- paper towels
- water
- "Keeping Track of Tails" data sheet

1) Choose ten different kinds of seeds. Draw a picture of each one on your data sheet.

2) Soak the seeds overnight.

3) Get the jar ready. Cut two paper towels to the right height to fit inside the jar. Wet the jar, then line it with the towels. The dampness should help the towels stick to the jar. Put 1 inch of water in the jar.

4) Carefully tuck each seed in between the towels and the jar near the top, and screw on the top of the jar.

5) Watch the seeds daily. Add a little water now and then to keep the jar moist. Draw the "tails" that you see developing on the seeds.

What's Happening?
The seeds soak up water and get soft. They burst open and send out roots and leaves. They can grow without soil because there is enough food in the seeds for germination.

Investigation

Keeping Track Of Tails

Draw and label each seed.

1. _____
2. _____
3. _____
4. _____
5. _____

6. _____
7. _____
8. _____
9. _____
10. _____

Measure and record the length of the "tails" (roots).

SEEDS:	1.	2.	3.	4.	5.	6.	7.	8.	9.	10.
SECOND DAY										
FOURTH DAY										
SIXTH DAY										
EIGHTH DAY										
TENTH DAY										

Which ones grow fastest? _____

Try leaving the jar in a dark place for two days.
What happens to the growth? _____

What can you conclude what seeds need for germination?

_____

_____

I grew!

Data Sheet

61

A Moldy Lesson

You can grow some interesting miniplants right on a piece of bread; no dirt is needed!

You need:
- 2 pieces of white bread
- cup of sand
- magnifying glass
- large needle
- jelly
- water
- plastic zip-up sandwich bags
- "Bread & Jelly Gardens" data sheet
- plastic zip-up gallon bags

1) Put one slice of bread on a paper plate. Sprinkle some water on the bread to get it moist. Seal it tightly in a plastic bag, and set it in a warm place. Watch it for a few days.

2) Put the sand on a paper plate. With the needle, carefully move some spores of mold to the sand. Seal this plate tightly in a plastic bag. Set it in a warm place and watch it for a few days. What has happened?

3) Also, put some of the mold spores on another piece of bread. Do not moisten the bread. Do not put it in a plastic bag.

Set this in a warm place and watch it for a few days. What happens?

4) Add some jelly to the dry sand, seal it in a plastic bag, and leave the plate in a warm spot. What happens?

What's Happening?
Mold needs food and moisture to grow. The mold won't grow on the dry sand because it can't make its own food. It must live off other things, such as the bread or the jelly. Neither will it live in a place that is dry, even if it has food.

Bread & Jelly Gardens

Draw what grew:

Moistened Bread	Dry Bread
Sand	Sand With Jelly

Explain what happened:

To the moist bread _____

To the dry bread _____

To the sand _____

To the sand and jelly _____

What does this mold need to grow? _____ ,

_____ , and _____ .

63

Data Sheet

Garden In A Soup Bowl

You can grow some unusual and beautiful plants in your lunch.
(But don't plan to eat the lunch!)

You need:
- can of tomato soup
- soup spoon
- 5 small bowls
- white bread
- plastic wrap
- rubber bands
- magnifying glass
- sticker labels
- tongue depressors
- "Don't Eat The Soup" data sheet

OUTTA SIGHT !

1) Label the bowls "1," "2," "3," "4," "5," and and put four spoonfuls of soup in each.

2) Plant some "seeds" in each bowl. Here's how:
   - Sneeze on bowl "1."
   - Use a wet tongue depressor to scrape some dirt off the floor for "2."
   - Use a tongue depressor to collect some dirt for outdoors for "3."
   - Sprinkle some bread crumbs on "4."
   - Scrape a wet tongue depressor across your arm for "5."

3) Cover each dish with plastic wrap and fasten with a rubber band. Set these in a warm place, and watch the gardens through a magnifying glass as they grow.

What's Happening?
The seeds you plant are "mold spores" and can be found almost everywhere. The spores are tiny plants which use the soup for food to grow and produce more plants.
You've collected different kinds of mold, so the plants will be different shapes and colors.

Investigation

64

Don't Eat The Soup!

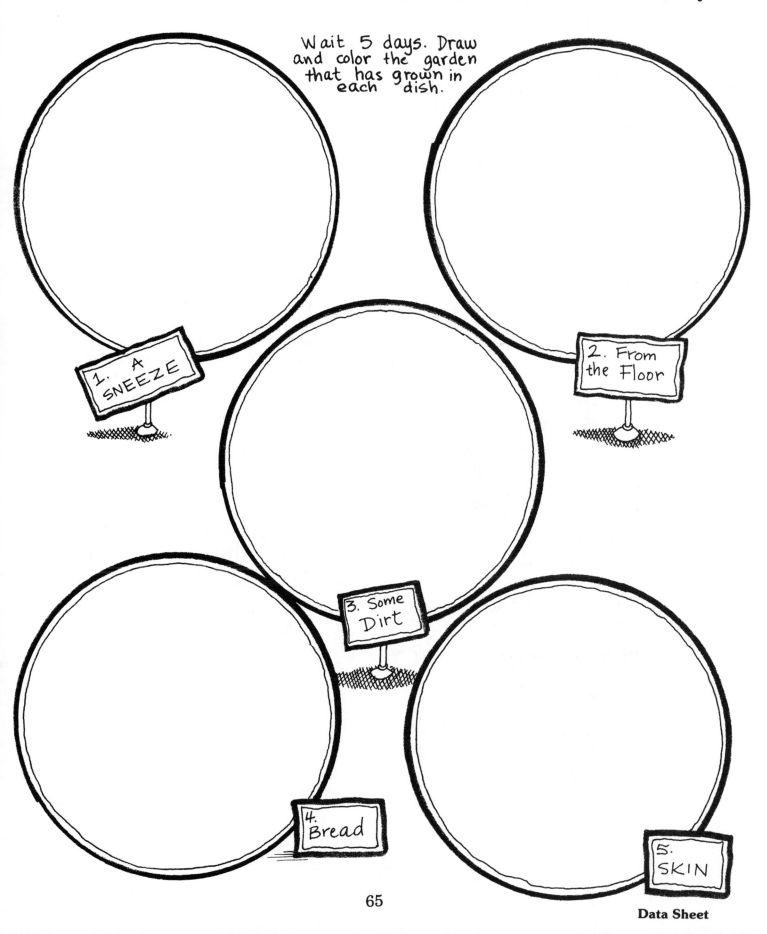

Wait 5 days. Draw and color the garden that has grown in each dish.

1. A SNEEZE

2. From the Floor

3. Some Dirt

4. Bread

5. SKIN

65

Create An Original Cactus

Take two cacti and switch their tops. Presto! You'll have two new plants with this marvelous trick called grafting.

You need:
- 2 small cacti, cylindrical-shaped and of similar diameters
- paper towels
- string
- clean, sharp knife
- rubbing alcohol
- adult helper

1) Tear off several sections of paper towels. Have these ready to cover the cacti any time you touch them. This will keep the spines out of your fingers.

2) Sterilize your knife by dipping it into rubbing alcohol. Be careful when handling the sharp knife. DO NOT TOUCH THE KNIFE BLADE at all. If you do, germs may get inside the cacti and keep the graft from working.

3) Cut off the top of each cactus with a straight cut across the cylinder.

4) Switch the tops. Line up the center sections, called piths, as closely as possible.

5) Press each top carefully but firmly onto the new bottom.

6) Tie string around each cactus to hold the new tops and bottoms together.

7) Keep the cacti in warm sunshine.

8) In about one month the grafts should be healed. Remove the strings and enjoy your original creations!

What's Happening?

The inner white portion of the cacti, the pith, is where the cactus growth takes place. When the pith of the top is lined up with the pith of the bottom, new cells are produced which pass food and water up and down through the plant. These cells connect to pass food and water and eventually will hold tight to each other. Combining parts of two different plants together is called "grafting."

Draw the two cacti before grafting.	Draw your two new plants here.

Investigation

Leaf Prints, Pressings, Pictures, and Papers

Look what you can do with a leaf!

You need:

- leaves
- waxed paper
- drawing paper
- construction paper
- yarn
- tempera paint
- iron
- paintbrush
- newspaper
- tissue paper
- rice paper
- white glue
- scissors
- water
- adult helper

PRINTS

1) Flatten the leaf well. Lay it upside down on newspaper.

2) Paint the underside (the side where the veins show best).

3) Carefully set the leaf, painted side down, on white drawing paper or colored construction paper.

4) Cover with another piece of paper, and press down firmly. Run your hand over the leaf from stem to tip.

5) Repeat with the same leaf or other leaves.

PRESSINGS

1) Place a leaf between pieces of waxed paper slightly larger than the leaf.

2) Place this in the middle of a heavy book and leave it for a week.

PAPERS

1) Collect a variety of small leaves.

2) Lay one or more on construction paper.

3) Cover the whole paper with tissue paper.

4) Paint the entire surface with a mixture of glue and water (1/2 glue, 1/2 water). (This will wrinkle some when you paint it.)

5) When it dries, you'll have lovely leaf paper for writing letters or wrapping gifts.

PICTURES

1) Arrange leaves in any design or picture between two pieces of waxed paper. Place this between pieces of newspaper.

2) Press with an iron set on medium heat.

3) Remove the waxed paper layers from the newspaper, and you'll have a see-through leaf picture.

4) Cut this into any shape you like, punch a hole in the top, string a piece of yarn through, and hang it in your window.

Investigation

What Will Rot? What Will Not?

Try planting some strange things, not to see how well they grow, but to learn how quickly they fall apart (decompose).

You need:
- outdoor garden or flowerpots
- spoons
- soil

Things to plant:
- 1/2 orange
- styrofoam cup
- plastic wrap
- bread slice
- bone
- small glass
- lettuce
- "Decomposition Report" data sheet

- sticky labels and pen
- newspaper

- aluminum foil
- apple core
- notebook
- paper
- small can
- paper cup
- plastic spoon
- cotton sock

1) Place each item in a 6 inch deep hole in the ground or in a flowerpot. Cover it with dirt, and label it with the item's name.

2) Pour 1 cup of water on each.

3) Water these every other day.

4) In four weeks dig them up, spread them on newspapers, and draw or write about what has happened to each one.

What's Happening?
Some of the things you planted are biodegradable. That means that molds, fungi, and bacteria in the soil will make these rot. These are the items that have begun to break down or fall apart in your experiment. Things not biodegradable will not break down in this way.

Decomposition Report

Use the space on the front and back of this paper to draw a picture of each item you dug up.

Next to the drawing, write the name of the item and a brief description of how it looks.

Also write a large "yes" if you found the item is biodegradable.

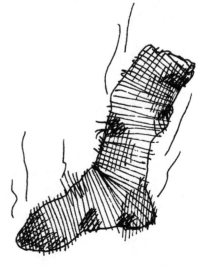

Data Sheet

How To Compost

Compost may look rotten, but it is actually good healthy stuff. Putting compost on soil gives minerals to new plants to make them bigger, stronger, and healthier. Here's a way to make compost for your garden. It's a good way to help your plants and recycle your garbage at the same time.

You need:

- small plastic garbage can with lid (preferably black)
- vegetable food scraps (no meat or bones)
- animals who like soil (pill bugs, worms, sow bugs)

- dead, rotting leaves
- soil
- bucket
- sharp knife
- water

1) Use the knife to poke small holes in the lid and around the sides of the garbage can. The holes should be large enough to let in air but too small for flies to get in.

2) Get some vegetable food scraps. Put an amount of dirt (about the same amount as the food scraps) in the bottom of the can. Add the food.

3) Add some dead, rotting leaves and a bunch of soil-loving bugs.

NO BONES ALLOWED! THANK GOODNESS!

SOIL

4) Stir this mixture with a large stick.

5) Keep this mixture moist but not wet. If it gets too dry, sprinkle in some water. If it gets too wet and sloppy, add dry dirt.

6) Keep the can outdoors in the sun. On very hot days, the temperature inside the can may get so hot that it kills the composting organisms. On these days, move the can into the shade.

7) Every day, add more food scraps, a few handfuls of dirt, a few sprinkles of water, and stir.

8) When the can is a little over half full, all the attention it needs is some stirring about twice a week.

9) In about one month, your compost will be finished! Try it on your garden or your houseplants, and see how they love it.

What's Happening?
Pill bugs, worms, and lots of tiny animals will eat your leftover potato peels, orange rinds, and other vegetables or fruit garbage. These creatures work together with molds, fungi, and bacteria in the soil to make the compost.

Lunch time?

Yummy!

Investigation

73

Make Friends With A Tree

Have you ever listened to a tree or hugged one? Getting to know a tree can be a grand new experience. Try it!

You need:
- a tree of your choice
- measuring tape
- typing paper
- pencil
- drawing paper
- crayons

1) Get close to your tree. Hug it and touch it with your hands, arms, face, and bare feet. Use your nose to learn about its smell. Walk around it for a long time and examine its bark, shape, colors, and movements.

2) Sit beside it, or climb it and sit in it for at least fifteen minutes. Listen and watch.

3) Do many of the things suggested on the next page. In time you should be pretty good friends with this tree.

BEHOLD, THE BEAUTIFUL, AWESOME, TREE!

- Collect its leaves or needles and seeds. Examine them. Make collages or leaf prints.

- Investigate the tree bark. Find a piece on the ground. Look at it with a magnifying glass.

- Keep a tree diary. Visit your tree regularly for a year. Each time you do, draw or write down things you see, hear, or smell.

- Paint a picture of your tree, or cut out a silhouette from black paper.

- Measure the tree once a month. Keep a record of the measurements.

- Start a tree scrapbook. Write everything you know about the tree, its approximate height, kind, measurements. Draw pictures of it in different seasons. Paste in samples of its leaves or needles, seeds, bark. Photograph yourself with it.

- Take a tape recorder to visit your tree. Sit quietly for fifteen minutes, and tape the sounds you hear in or near the tree.

- Have a live animal watch one day. Visit the tree just for the purpose of finding out what animals live there. Use a magnifying glass to help you.

- Perform a tree rubbing. Tack a piece of typing paper to the tree's bark. With a dark crayon or soft pencil, rub lightly over the paper. Keep rubbing until the pattern appears on your paper.

- Have a tree party. Invite friends to come sit under your tree. Serve tea and cookies, and tell them what's special about your tree. Ask them to share their special trees with you, too.

- Write a book, poem, or song about your tree.

Investigation

Striped Celery?

Have you ever eaten striped celery? Try some! It will help you learn how some plants get a drink when they're thirsty.

You need:
- freshly cut white flowers such as daisies or carnations
- leafy celery
- tall glasses or jars
- water
- red and blue food coloring
- kitchen knife

1) Fill two glasses with water. Put red food coloring in one and blue in the other. Cut a slice off the ends of the freshest flowers and celery. Put the flowers in the blue water and the celery in the red water.

2) Look at these the next day. Cut a piece of celery in slices to see the tiny veins. What has happened?

What's Happening?
The water travels up the stalk to the leaves or petals through tiny tubes called "xylem." This upward movement of water is called "capillary action."

Investigation

76

Physical Sciences

In The Bag

A state might be something you live in. But there are other kinds of states. This investigation will help you get to know three important states where no one lives.

You need:
* 3 plastic zip-up bags
* small block of wood
* 1 cup water
* drinking glass
* ruler
* "What Manner Of Matter?" data sheet

1) Put the block of wood in one bag and a cup of water in another bag. Blow air into the third bag and zip it shut quickly.

2) Use the data sheet to guide you in examining the contents of each bag

and answering some questions about it.

3) After you finish, draw your own conclusions about the three states of matter.

What's Happening?
Most solids are visible, do not change shape easily, and do not allow a solid object to be passed through them easily. Most liquids are visible, do change shape easily, and do allow a solid object to be moved through them easily. Most gases are not visible, do change shape very easily, and do allow a solid object to pass through them easily.

What Manner of Matter?

WOOD — Solid

Can it be seen easily?_____

Can you move the ruler through it? ____

Does it change shape easily? _____

What can you conclude about solids?

_____

_____

_____

WATER — Liquid

Can it be seen easily? _____

Move and squeeze the bag gently, put the bag into a glass, and lay it flat on the table. Does it change shape easily? _____

Open the bag and put a ruler through the water. Can you do this easily?_____

What can you conclude about liquids?

_____

_____

_____

AIR — Gas

Can you see it easily? _____

Move and squeeze the bag gently, then put it in a glass. Lay it flat on the table. Does the air change shape easily?_____

Open the bag and put a ruler through the air. Can you do this easily? _____

What can you conclude about gases?

_____

_____

_____

Data Sheet

Ready For A Change

To be a good scientist, you need to know about two different kinds of changes and be able to figure out when each kind happens.

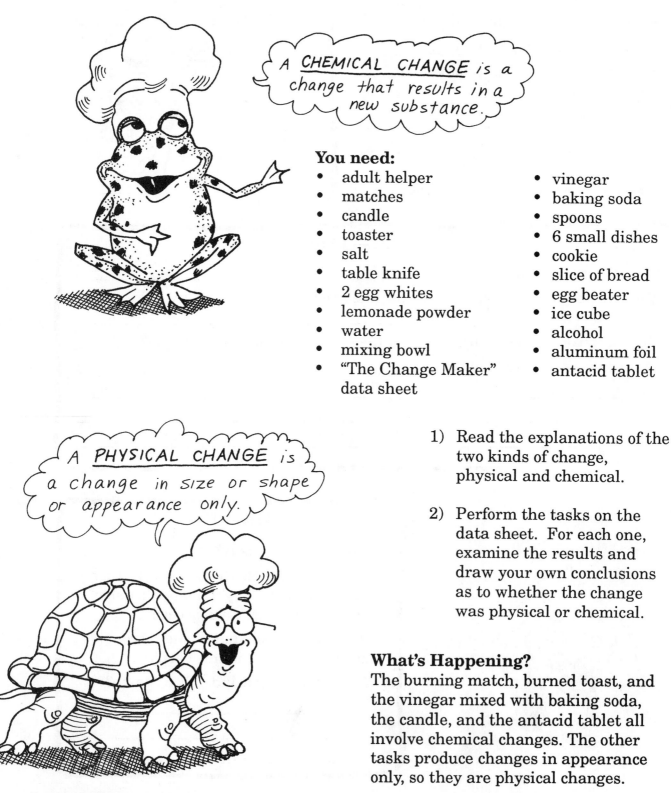

A CHEMICAL CHANGE is a change that results in a new substance.

You need:
- adult helper
- matches
- candle
- toaster
- salt
- table knife
- 2 egg whites
- lemonade powder
- water
- mixing bowl
- "The Change Maker" data sheet

- vinegar
- baking soda
- spoons
- 6 small dishes
- cookie
- slice of bread
- egg beater
- ice cube
- alcohol
- aluminum foil
- antacid tablet

A PHYSICAL CHANGE is a change in size or shape or appearance only.

1) Read the explanations of the two kinds of change, physical and chemical.

2) Perform the tasks on the data sheet. For each one, examine the results and draw your own conclusions as to whether the change was physical or chemical.

What's Happening?
The burning match, burned toast, and the vinegar mixed with baking soda, the candle, and the antacid tablet all involve chemical changes. The other tasks produce changes in appearance only, so they are physical changes.

Investigation

The Change Maker

Dr. Struedel is making changes. Repeat his experiments and observe what happens. Put an "x" in each box below that describes the result. Then decide what kind of change occurred. Write "P" for physical changes and "C" for chemical changes.

I'M GOING TO CHANGE A FEW THINGS AROUND HERE!

Physical or Chemical?	CHANGES ▶	SIZE or SHAPE	APPEARANCE	SUBSTANCE
	Mix Vinegar + Baking Soda			
	Burn a match			
	Toast bread until it's burned			
	Mix lemonade + water			
	Melt an ice cube			
	Burn a wax candle			
	Set a few drops of water in a dish overnight			
	Set a few drops of alcohol in a dish overnight			
	Crumple a square of foil into a ball			
	Beat egg whites 7 minutes			
	Slice a cookie in 4 pieces			
	Drop antacid tablet in water			

Data Sheet

Pop Secret Science

The next time you're hungry for popcorn, take a closer look at what happens when it gets popped!

You need:
- adult helper
- test tube
- short candle and matches
- metal tongs
- unpopped popcorn

- tongue depressor
- cooking oil
- eyedropper
- aluminum foil
- "As The Corn Pops" data sheet

1) Set the candle on aluminum foil.

2) Put a drop of cooking oil and one popcorn seed in the test tube. Cover it with an aluminum foil circle.

3) Light the candle and hold it above the flame at an angle pointed away from everyone's face. Do not let the test tube touch the flame.

4) Move the test tube back and forth so the seed doesn't burn.

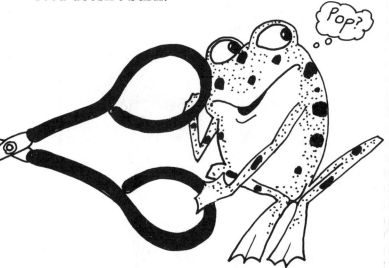

5) When the seed pops, put out the flame and let it cool. Remove the seed with the tongue depressor. Complete the data sheet questions.

What's Happening?
Each seed contains moisture which turns to steam when heated. The steam puts pressure on the outside cover of the seed (called a seed coat) and causes it to burst. If the seed is cracked or dried out, the moisture escapes easily and it won't pop.

Investigation

82

As The Corn Pops

Draw the unpopped seed here.

What do you think will happen when the seed is heated? _____

_____

Why will this happen? _____

_____

Draw the seed after it was heated.

Examine the inside of the aluminum foil cover.

What do you find? _____

Draw a conclusion about why the corn popped.

_____

_____

_____

Don't forget to make some popcorn to eat!

Data Sheet

Roll Me Some Ice Cream

Hungry for some ice cream? Here's an easy way to make it by rolling a can around on the floor.

ICE CREAM Recipe

Mix together well:
1½ C half and half
2 tsp vanilla
¼ C sugar

You need:

- a friend
- 1 lb coffee can with lid
- 3 lb coffee can with lid
- sturdy rubber band
- plastic wrap
- paper cups
- plastic spoons
- measuring spoons and cups
- crushed ice
- box of salt
- mixing bowl and spoon
- vanilla
- whipping cream
- sugar

1) Mix the ice cream mixture. Pour it into the small can. The can should be about 3/4 full. If it isn't, you can stir in more whipping cream.

2) Put the top on tightly. Cover it with a piece of plastic wrap held by a rubber band.

3) Set the small can in the center of the large can. Put a layer of ice about 2 inches thick in the bottom of the can around the small can. Then sprinkle 1/4 cup of salt on top of the ice.

4) Continue layering the ice and salt until the can is almost full. Put the top on the can.

Freeze the ice cream.

1) Sit on the floor and roll the can back and forth to a friend.

2) In fifteen minutes check the ice cream by carefully opening the inside can. Be careful not to get any of the salt water in the ice cream.

3) When the ice cream is frozen, get busy eating it!

What's Happening?

Adding salt to ice lowers the freezing temperature of the water. The freezing temperature around the small can then is lower-than-normal freezer temperature, so the ice cream mixture freezes faster than it would in the freezer. Slow freezing would cause large ice crystals to form, but this faster freezing keeps the mixture creamy. By rolling the can back and forth, the mixture is constantly mixed and circulated against the cold sides of the can. In addition to keeping the ice cream in contact with the low temperature of the ice outside, this circulating also mixes air into the ice cream and helps make it fluffy.

ICE

Valley Bros.
Coffee

Lid

SALT

3 pounds

85

Investigation

Ask Your Freezer

Which freezes faster, cold or hot water? Let your freezer help you find out.

You need:
- adult helper
- teakettle
- water
- stove
- timer or watch
- 2 small sturdy plastic containers
- measuring cup
- marker
- freezer

1) Label one container "hot," and the other "cold."

2) Pour 1/3 cup boiling water into one container and 1/3 cup cold water into the other.

3) Set both containers on a flat surface inside your freezer.

4) Check after a half hour. Then keep checking every five minutes to see which container freezes first.

5) Write down the time it takes for each one to freeze.

What's Happening?
Surprise! The boiling water freezes first. Both samples freeze at freezing temperature, 32° F. But the hot water freezes first because hot water evaporates faster than cold. While it was hot, more of the water evaporated leaving less water in the container, so it froze faster.

Investigation

Wonderful, Glorious Goop

It acts like a liquid. It acts like a solid. Which is it? Whichever it is, it's sure fun!

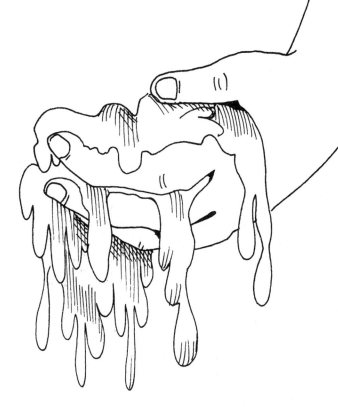

You need:
- cornstarch
- water
- food coloring
- bowl
- spoon
- measuring cups and spoons

1) Measure 1/2 cup cornstarch into a bowl.

2) Add 1/4 cup plus 1 tablespoon water, and mix in. It will be very hard to stir, but keep working at it.

3) Stir in a few drops of food coloring. This will take a while to mix in, too.

4) Now you're ready to "play" with your glorious goop.

What's Happening?
The cornstarch and water did not form a solution. The solid particles are held up by the water molecules but not dissolved in them. This is called a "suspension." Squeezing keeps the suspension together and it feels solid. When you stop squeezing, the liquid and solid begin to come apart and the goop starts to feel like liquid.

Squeeze it — how does it feel?
Roll it into a ball.
Roll it into a snake — what happens? Break it apart.
Stop squeezing. Just let it lay on your hands.
What happens?

87

Investigation

Great Gooey Gumdrops

Here's a tasty way to learn something about suspensions and eat them, too!

You need:
- package of any flavor gelatin
- eyedropper
- small cereal bowl
- bowl of cool water
- fork

1) Pour the package of gelatin into the cereal bowl.

2) Use the eyedropper to pick up one drop of water and squeeze it into the center of the gelatin.

3) When the water has disappeared into the gelatin, squeeze another drop on the same place.

4) Keep squeezing one drop at a time on the gelatin. Make sure you squeeze water on the same place each time and wait until the water is absorbed by the gelatin.

5) After you've squeezed about eight drops, use a fork to pick up the lump that's formed. You'll have your first, gooey gumdrop.

6) Pile up the dry gelatin that remains, and start over again for more!

What's Happening?
Gelatin holds the water in between its molecules. A liquid suspended in (or held within) a solid in this way is called a "suspension."

Mmmmm Yummy!

Gelatin Gumdrops

Eggs That Bounce

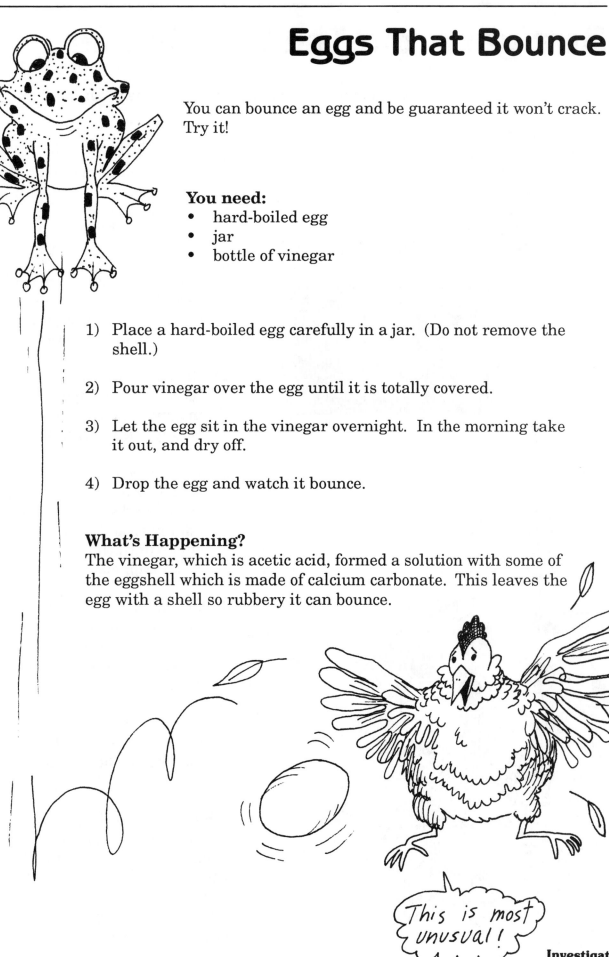

You can bounce an egg and be guaranteed it won't crack. Try it!

You need:
- hard-boiled egg
- jar
- bottle of vinegar

1) Place a hard-boiled egg carefully in a jar. (Do not remove the shell.)

2) Pour vinegar over the egg until it is totally covered.

3) Let the egg sit in the vinegar overnight. In the morning take it out, and dry off.

4) Drop the egg and watch it bounce.

What's Happening?
The vinegar, which is acetic acid, formed a solution with some of the eggshell which is made of calcium carbonate. This leaves the egg with a shell so rubbery it can bounce.

This is most unusual!

Investigation

Straight From The Salt Shaker

You can make salt disappear and reappear again.

You need:
- salt shaker
- black paper
- magnifying glass
- small pot
- small jar with lid
- "A Salty Question" data sheet

- water
- aluminum foil
- spoon
- heat source
- adult helper

1) Have your data sheet ready to record your observations and conclusions as you perform the following investigations.

2) Shake a few grains of salt onto a piece of black paper. Use a magnifying glass to examine them closely. Draw what you see.

3) Put a spoonful of salt into a jar. Add a spoonful of water. Put on the lid and shake the jar. Keep adding spoonfuls of water and shake until the water is clear. What happens to the salt?

4) Put a drop of this salt water onto a piece of aluminum foil, and let it sit until the water is gone. Heat a small amount of the salt water in the pot.

5) Use a magnifying glass to examine the leftovers from the aluminum foil and the heated pot.

What's Happening?
The salt dissolved in the water, making a solution. But salt was left when the water evaporated. Since the salt was always there, this process (called "recovering a solute") is a physical change.

A Salty Question

Draw the magnified salt grains here.

What do you predict will happen when you mix salt with water in the jar? _____

_____

Add a spoonful of salt to the water and shake the jar.

What happens? _____

Use the magnifying glass to examine the leftovers on the aluminum foil and in the pot.

How does it look? _____

How does it taste? _____

Which method of recovering the solute was faster? _____

_____

What conclusions can you draw from this investigation?

_____

_____

Data Sheet

It's Crystal Clear

When you stir salt into hot water, where does the salt go? It seems to disappear, but you can get it back.

You will need:
- salt or sea salt
- sugar
- Epsom salts
- laundry detergent flakes
- 4 glass jars
- 4 spoons
- magnifying glass
- thread or thin string
- very hot water
- pencils
- paper clips
- food coloring
- "Crystals On A String" data sheet

1) Fill a jar half full of very hot water. Stir in a cup or more of salt, a little at a time, until no more will dissolve.

2) Rub some salt onto a piece of string. Tie it around a pencil, tie a paper clip to the other end, and drop it into the water. Lay the pencil across the jar.

3) Put the glass in a cool place where it won't be disturbed. Do not touch the jar or the pencil. Watch for a few days.

4) Repeat the process with Epsom salts, sugar, and laundry detergent flakes. Try adding a little food coloring to one of the solutions.

What's Happening?
The salt dissolves in the hot water. But cold water can't hold as much salt in a dissolved form. So as the water cools, the salt forms again on the string.

Crystals On A String

Use a magnifying glass to look at the results of your experiments. Draw what you see.

salt crystals	sugar crystals
Epsom salt crystals	laundry detergent flakes

Which ones grew largest? _____

Talk about how the crystals are different.

You can eat the sugar crystals!

93

Crystals Good Enough To Eat

Here's a way to make your own rock candy. You'll discover that science never tasted so good!

You need:
- an adult helper
- heavy cooking pot
- heat source
- hot pad
- wooden spoon
- 2 small glass jars
- 2 tongue depressors
- sugar
- water
- food coloring

1) Mix 2 1/4 cups sugar with 1 cup water in the cooking pot. The sugar may not completely dissolve until the mixture is heated.

2) With help from an adult, heat the mixture over medium heat until it boils.

3) Let it boil for two minutes without stirring it.

4) Meanwhile get the glass jars warm by filling them with hot water. Empty and dry them out.

5) Carefully and slowly pour half the mixture into each jar.

6) Add two drops of food coloring to each jar, and stir with a tongue depressor.

7) Leave the tongue depressors in the jars and let them stand for about a week.

Do not touch or disturb the glass or move the sticks.

8) When crystals have collected on the sticks, the rock candy is ready. Pick up the sticks and enjoy!

Note: After a few days, if a crust forms on top of the water, carefully break it so the water can continue to evaporate.

Crystals good enough to eat!

What's Happening?
The mixture you made had too much sugar for the amount of water. It didn't dissolve until the water was heated. This is called a supersaturated solution. Crystals will grow from a supersaturated solution. As the water evaporates slowly, crystals will form around a small object put into the solution. The molecules in the sugar join together arranging themselves in a particular organized shape. This is what makes crystals.

Investigation

The Mysterious, Disappearing Liquid

Mix these two liquids together, and watch something quite unusual happen.

You need:
- 2 cups rubbing alcohol
- 2 cups water
- large spoon
- measuring cup
- 2 large bowls or pots

1) Mix exactly 2 cups rubbing alcohol and 2 cups water together in one bowl or pot. Stir well.

2) Use the measuring cup to measure this mixture carefully. As you measure each cup, pour it into the other bowl or pot.

3) 2 + 2 = 4, right? Did you measure four cups? You may want to measure it again to see if you were right. What do you think has happened? What explanations might you give for this strange result?

What's Happening?
Water molecules are smaller than alcohol molecules, so they are able to "sneak" in the spaces between the alcohol molecules. In separate cups, each liquid measures two cups. But together the water "sneaks" around the alcohol molecules so that the measurement equals less than four cups. The mixture appears to have shrunk!

Investigation

The Amazing, Changing Liquid

Surprise your friends with this magic trick to turn punch into plain, ordinary water.

You need:
- laundry bleach
- red food coloring
- spoon
- measuring spoons
- water
- 2 clear glasses of the same size
- an audience

1) Before the audience arrives, set up the trick. Make "punch" by filling one glass 3/4 full with water and stirring in three drops of red food color.

2) In the second glass, put 1 tablespoon of bleach, nothing else. It won't be noticed by your audience. The glass will look empty.

3) Invite some friends to watch your trick. Tell them you will change the punch into water.

4) Pour the punch into the "empty" glass. Wait a few minutes, and "Presto!" The "punch" will turn into clear water.

5) CAUTION: Do not drink the punch!

What's Happening?
Laundry bleach contains sodium chlorite, a compound that contains chlorine. Water is made up of hydrogen and oxygen. The hydrogen in the water combines with the chlorine in the bleach. This frees the oxygen in the water to combine with the food coloring, making a colorless substance that looks like clear water.

Investigation

Invisible Inks

When you need to send a very secret message, write it in one of these invisible inks.

You need:
- adult helper
- lemon juice
- orange juice
- small paintbrush
- pen
- toothpicks
- milk
- vinegar
- paper
- iron or lamp

To Write The Message
1) Write a "decoy" message with the pen. Leave large spaces between the lines for writing the actual message.

2) Dip the paintbrush or toothpicks in any of the liquids. Write the real message between the lines of the fake one.

3) When the ink is dry, the message can be sent.

To Read The Message
The person receiving the message should iron the paper with a medium-hot iron or warm the paper over a light bulb. The secret message will magically appear!

What's Happening?
These liquids contain carbon. When they are heated, the heat causes a chemical change. It breaks apart the juice, and the carbon is freed to show its true color which is dark.

Investigation

Fizzy Drinks

This is just what you need on a hot day, a fizzy drink you can stir up in a matter of minutes. And you'll get a science lesson at the same time!

You need:
- baking soda
- citric acid crystals (from the drugstore)
- lemonade
- orange juice
- 2 drinking glasses
- powdered sugar
- ice cubes
- teaspoon
- tablespoon
- small bowl

Orange Fizz

1) Mix together 2 tablespoons powdered sugar, 2 tablespoons citric acid crystals, and 1 tablespoon baking soda in a bowl. Use the spoon to mash them together into a powder.

2) Put 1 tablespoon of the mixture into a glass. Add two ice cubes. Pour in orange juice, stir quickly.

3) Drink immediately before the bubbles disappear.

Lemon Fizz

1) Mix 1/2 teaspoon baking soda, 2 ice cubes, and a half glass of lemonade. Stir quickly.
2) Drink immediately before the bubbles disappear.

What's Happening?
The baking soda (sodium bicarbonate) reacts with the citric acid in the crystals and in the lemonade to produce the gas carbon dioxide. The gas bubbles make the drink fizzy.

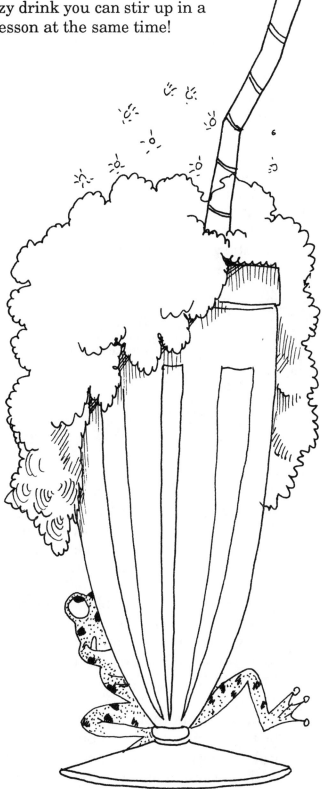

Investigation

The Magic Color Switch

It's magic! You can turn blue into red right before their eyes.

You need:
- ammonia mixed with water
  (equal amounts)
- tincture of iodine
- laxative pills
- rubbing alcohol
- medicine dropper
- cotton swabs
- small dish
- 2 small jars
- white typing paper
- paper towels
- "Mystery Messages" data sheet

What's Happening?

The starch in the typing paper combined with iodine in "Ink B" to form a blue compound, so the drawing looked blue. Ammonia and iodine form a colorless compound. That's why the ammonia wipe made the blue drawing disappear. Phenolphthalein, a substance in the laxative in "Ink A," is an indicator that turns pink in the presence of a base. Ammonia is a base.

1) Make the magic inks. (See recipes on page 101.) Dip a cotton swab into "Ink A" and draw a large, happy, smiling face on the white paper. Let it dry. The drawing will disappear.

2) Gather your audience. Show them the blank paper. Tell them a story about a girl who was very sad and blue. Use a new cotton swab to draw a large, sad face with "Ink B." The ink will look blue.

3) Now tell them that you have the power to wipe away this blue girl's unhappiness. Get a paper towel damp with the ammonia/water mixture, and wipe it across the blue drawing. A pink, happy face will magically appear!

Investigation

Mystery Messages

Use a cotton swab and magic "INK A" to write a secret message to a friend. Write in large, clear letters. Let the message dry.

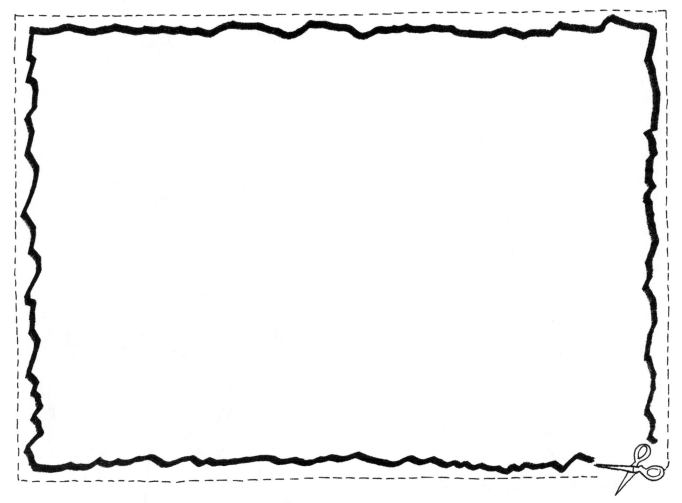

Now, use "INK B" to write a message that is not secret, one that anyone could see. Cut it out and pass the message. When the message is received, the secret one can be read after it is wiped with a paper towel dipped in the ammonia/water mixture.

MAGIC INK A

Mash two pieces of laxative in a small dish. Add some rubbing alcohol and mix. Let this sit five minutes. Then transfer the liquid to a jar with the dropper.

MAGIC INK B

Put a few tablespoons of water in a jar. Add a few drops of iodine until it looks like tea. It should look blue when you write with it.

Data Sheet

Homemade Rockets & Jet Boats

Try these jet-propelled toys you can make in a matter of minutes, right in your own kitchen or classroom.

You need:
- plastic bottle with screw-on top
- glass bottle with cork top
- paper towels
- vinegar
- baking soda
- straight pins
- water
- drinking straw
- scissors
- chunk of plastic clay
- crepe, tissue paper, or ribbons
- paint or stickers (optional)
- sink or bathtub full of water

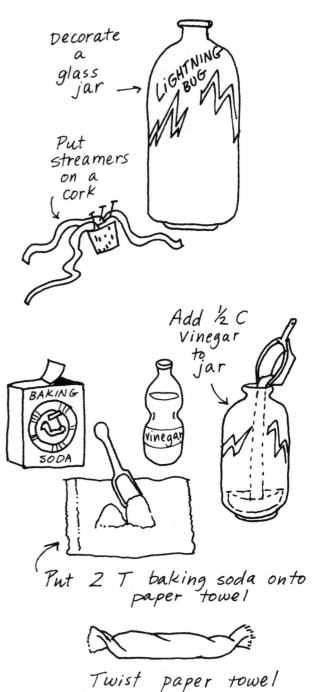

Decorate a glass jar →

Put streamers on a cork

Add ½ C vinegar to jar

Put 2 T baking soda onto paper towel

Twist paper towel

Rocket

1) Decorate the glass bottle with paint or stickers.

2) Use straight pins to attach bright strips of paper or ribbon to the cork.

3) Pour 1/2 cup vinegar into the bottle.

4) Cut a 5 inch square of paper towel. Pour 2 tablespoons baking soda into the center. Roll up the paper and twist the ends.

5) Get the cork wet.

6) Drop the rolled-up paper into the bottle. Quickly put the cork in the bottle, stand back, and watch your rocket launch.

Investigation

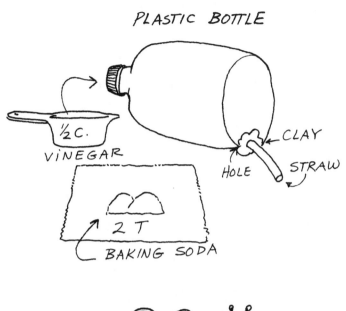

PLASTIC BOTTLE

½ C.

VINEGAR

CLAY

HOLE

STRAW

2 T

BAKING SODA

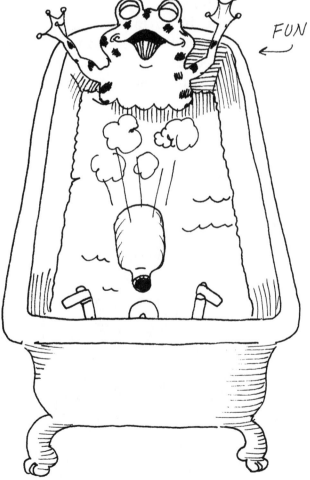

FUN

1) Decorate the plastic bottle with paint or stickers.

2) Poke a small hole in the bottom corner of the bottle.

3) Push the straw in the hole, slanting it down so it will be under water when the bottle is placed in water.

4) Put clay around the straw to seal the hole.

5) Pour 1/2 cup vinegar into the bottle.

6) Cut a 5 inch square from a paper towel. Pour 2 tablespoons baking soda in the center.

7) Roll up the paper towel and twist the ends to hold it shut.

8) Push the rolled-up paper into the bottle. Quickly screw on the top. Set the jet boat in a sink or tub of water with the straw pointing down, and watch it go!

What's Happening?

As the vinegar soaks into the paper towel, it mixes with the baking soda. Baking soda, a chemical called sodium bicarbonate, reacts with vinegar to produce a gas called carbon dioxide. The molecules in gas move faster and push each other apart. This causes pressure to build up in the rocket and the boat. The pressure launches the cork rocket and escapes out the straw to propel the boat.

Investigation

Jumping Mothballs & Dancing Raisins

Watch some science magic that can make mothballs and raisins "perform" unusual dances! Then see if you can figure out how it happened.

You need:
- 2 tall olive jars without labels
- a tablespoon
- baking soda
- white vinegar
- raisins
- mothballs

1) Fill a jar half full with water.

2) Stir in 2 tablespoons of baking soda.

3) Drop in five raisins.

4) Add 2 tablespoons of vinegar, and watch what happens. Can you explain why they're dancing?

5) What do you think will happen if you attempt this with mothballs? Try it.

What's Happening?
When vinegar and baking soda combine, they produce a gas called carbon dioxide. That's what the bubbles are. The bubbles collect on the raisins (or mothballs) and rise to the surface taking the raisins (or mothballs) along. Then the bubbles escape at the surface and drop the raisins (or mothballs), which fall until they collect more bubbles. Then they rise again and "keep on dancing"!

The Invisible Muscle

Here's how to make a gas that has amazing strength.

You need:
- cookie sheet
- tall, clear glass
- vinegar
- baking soda
- measuring cup and spoons
- eyedropper
- match
- small bottle with a push-on plastic cap

1) Set the glass on the cookie sheet. Put 2 tablespoons of baking soda and 1/3 cup vinegar into the glass. You've made a gas called carbon dioxide. Can you see it?

2) What do you think will happen if you make carbon dioxide in a closed bottle? Put some baking soda into the bottle. Use the eyedropper to add some vinegar. Very quickly put the cap on the bottle. Watch what happens.

3) Right away hold a lit match next to the bubbles and you can learn something else about carbon dioxide.

What's Happening?
The vinegar and baking soda combine to make carbon dioxide. The molecules of the gas spread far apart and force the top right off the bottle. Carbon dioxide puts the match out because it takes the place of air which contains the oxygen the match needs to burn.

Investigation

105

Ever-So-Yummy Meringues

Here's a way to study science and eat it, too!

You need:
- adult helper
- 4 eggs
- 3/4 cup superfine sugar
- food coloring
- 1/2 teaspoon cream of tartar
- 1/2 teaspoon vanilla
- metal mixing bowl
- large brown paper bag
- rubber spatula
- large spoon
- scissors
- electric mixer or egg beater
- oven

1) Let eggs sit out for about a half hour to warm.

2) Preheat oven to 250°.

3) Cut the paper bag to cover each cookie sheet.

4) Separate the egg whites from the yolks. Put the whites in the metal bowl.

5) Add the cream of tartar, and beat the egg whites until they're foamy. Continue beating them adding sugar one spoonful at a time. Add a drop or two of food coloring, too.

6) Beat the egg whites until they are stiff and glossy.

7) Drop the mixture in swirly heaps onto the cookie sheets, and bake at 250° for one hour or until they are light brown.

Investigation

106

8) After one hour, turn off the oven and open it. Leave the meringues in the oven for another hour.

9) When the meringues are completely cool, remove them from the cookie sheet and examine them. How are they different from the raw egg whites?

10) Enjoy eating your experiment!

What's Happening?
Whipping egg whites changes the shape of the protein molecules and allows them to trap air and puff up. Cream of tartar is an acid that helps keep air trapped longer in the egg whites. This is what makes the mixture stiff. The heat in your oven causes the trapped air to expand and make the meringues even puffier. The heat also causes the egg whites to change from liquid to a crispy solid. This is a process called "coagulation."

Meringue

Investigation

107

Quick & Easy Bath Salts

Learn about chemical changes while you enjoy a nice soapy soak in your bathtub.

You need:
- baking soda
- perfume
- 2 bowls
- large spoon
- food coloring
- measuring cup
- rolling pin
- glass jar with lid
- heavy plastic bag
- water

1) Dig into the bottom of the box of baking soda with a spoon and get some big chunks. Put these into the plastic bag and roll the bag to crush the soda into small lumps.

2) Pour half the lumps into each bowl. Add a few drops of color to each bowl, and stir until all the soda picks up some color.

3) Wait 15 minutes for the soda to dry. Then mix the colors together and put them into a tightly closed jar.

4) Test the bath salts by putting a spoonful in a bowl of water. How does it feel? Compare it to the feel of plain water.

5) The next time you take a bath, dump a handful of bath salts into the tub to make the water feel this way.

What's Happening?
Baking soda is a chemical called sodium carbonate. The carbonate combines with calcium in hard water and forms calcium carbonate. This new compound makes the water feel "soft." Soap is much soapier in soft water and lathers more easily.

Take Your Money To The Cleaners

Borrow some dirty pennies from your piggy bank for this interesting experiment.

You need:
- drinking glass
- white vinegar
- water
- salt
- measuring spoons
- paper towels
- dirty pennies

1) Mix 1 tablespoon salt and 4 tablespoons vinegar in the glass.

2) Drop in some dirty pennies, and watch what happens!

3) Wash off the pennies with water, and dry them on paper towels.

What's Happening?
Vinegar is a chemical called acetic acid. Salt is the chemical sodium chloride. When these two chemicals mix, they react to form a small amount of a new chemical called hydrochloric acid. This acid has the ability to shine your copper pennies instantly.

Laundry day!

White Vinegar

Investigation

109

What's Wrong With My Banana?

Did you ever wonder why banana slices turn brown?
Do some investigating, and you'll find out.

You need:
- water
- 2 plates or trays
- a small mixing bowl and spoon
- measuring cup
- chewable vitamin C pills
- sharp knife
- adult help
- foods listed on the "Oxidation Investigation" data sheet
- "Oxidation Investigation" data sheet

1) Crush a vitamin C pill with a spoon, and add 1 cup of water. Stir until the pill is dissolved.

2) Cut two slices of each fruit or vegetable. Lay one slice of each on one plate.

3) Take another slice of each, dip it in the vitamin C liquid, and lay it on the second plate.

4) Let the trays sit out uncovered for two hours. Watch what happens to the foods. Record your observations on the data sheet.

What's Happening?
Oxygen in the air is an element that reacts with substances in the fruits and vegetables in a process called oxidation. When foods oxidize, some turn brown. Foods containing vitamin C or foods dipped in vitamin C do not oxidize quickly. Vitamin C is an antioxidant, a substance that slows or stops oxidation.

Oxidation Investigation

My prediction about what will happen to the foods on tray 1:

_____

My prediction about tray 2 (foods dipped in vitamin C):

_____

What Happened?	(Tray #1)	(Tray #2)
TOMATO		
APPLE		
ORANGE		
PEACH		
BANANA		
LETTUCE		
LEMON		
PEAR		
OTHERS		

From these investigations, I can conclude:

_____

_____

_____

Data Sheet

Please Don't Eat The Molecules

A chemical formula tells you exactly what a substance contains. Some minimarshmallows can be the atoms you put together to show what the formulas mean. But don't eat the molecules, just the leftover marshmallows!

Symbols

Al	Aluminum
C	Carbon
Ca	Calcium
Cl	Chlorine
Cu	Copper
Fe	Iron
H	Hydrogen
He	Helium
K	Potassium
Mn	Manganese
Na	Sodium
O	Oxygen

You need:
- colored miniature marshmallows
- toothpicks
- fine-point permanent markers
- "What's In A Name?" data sheet

1) Review the symbols for some of the elements on the chart below. Also, read the clues for naming compounds on the data sheet.

2) The formula for water is H_2O. Use the marker to write "H" (for hydrogen) on two marshmallows of

the same color. Write "O" for oxygen on one marshmallow of a different color. Then connect the marshmallow "atoms" to show how water is made of two hydrogen atoms and one oxygen atom.

3) The formula for carbon dioxide is CO_2. Make a molecule for carbon dioxide. Remember to label each "atom" with its symbol.

4) Write the formulas, and make the molecules for the compounds shown on the data sheet.

Investigation

What's In A Name?

Name this compound. _____

What is the formula? _____

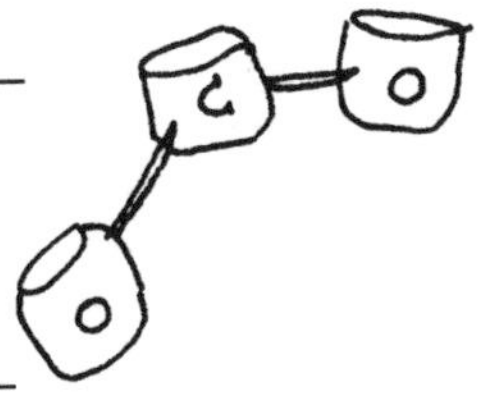

Write the missing formula or name for each of these. Then use marshmallows and toothpicks to represent the molecule.

NAME	FORMULA
sulphur trioxide	_____
_____	CO
sodium chloride	_____
copper dioxide	_____
_____	HCL
_____	K_2O_3
_____	MnO_2

NOW DON'T EAT ALL THE MARSHMALLOWS!

CLUES

- Compounds ending in "ide" have two elements in the name.
- The "little" numbers tell how many atoms there are of that element.
- A prefix "mono" means one atom of that element, "di" means two, "tri" means three.

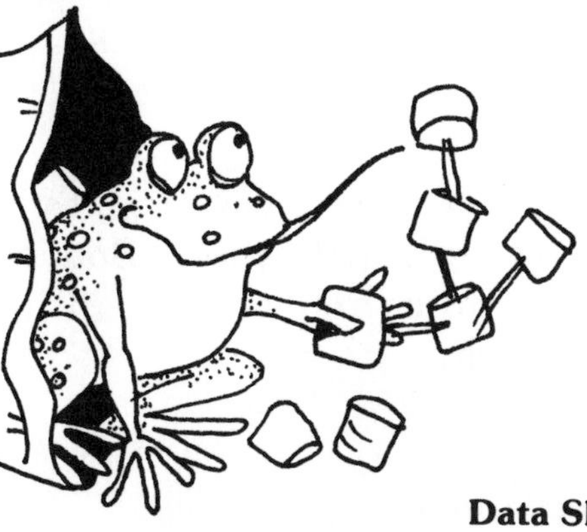

Data Sheet

113

Purple Cabbage Chemistry

Cook up some purple cabbage and work some color-changing magic on some ordinary stuff from your kitchen.

Wonderful! A scientific experiment — and lunch, too!

You need:
- cooking pot
- water
- stove
- 1/2 purple cabbage
- grater
- coffee filter or a sieve
- large jar with top
- several baby food jars
- large bowl
- labels for jars
- pen
- spoons or medicine droppers
- "The Acid Test" data sheet

1) Grate the cabbage into the pot and cover it with water. Boil it for five minutes and let it sit until the juice is dark.

2) Cool and strain it through the filter or sieve into the bowl. Transfer the liquid to the big jar. (You can eat the cabbage.)

3) Place small amounts of several substances (see data sheet) into jars and mix in a few drops of the purple juice. The "magic" juice will change color!

What's Happening?
The cabbage juice is an indicator. It indicates the presence of an acid or a base. It will turn pink in the presence of acids and green or blue in the presence of bases.

The Acid Test

Test each substance with cabbage juice. Tell what color the indicator became, and check each one "acid" or "base."

	color	acid	base
SALT			
SOAP SHAVINGS			
MILK			
LEMON JUICE			
BAKING POWDER			
BLACK TEA			
FIZZY COLA			
LIME JUICE			
LAUNDRY SOAP POWDER			
MILK OF MAGNESIA®			
TUMS®			
TOOTHPASTE			
SHAMPOO			
VINEGAR			
ORANGE JUICE			

Blue cabbage is also yummy!

Try mixing cabbage juice with 1 tablespoon of lemon juice. Add 1 tablespoon of baking soda. What color does the liquid become?

_____

Explain why _____

_____

_____

Add some other substances to your chart and give them "The Acid Test."

Data Sheet

Ask The Iodine

Starch is one of the items our bodies need to get from the food we eat. Here is a way to test foods to find some good sources of starch.

You need:
- small bits of each food listed on data sheet
- newspapers
- eyedropper
- iodine
- adult helper
- "Starch Search" data sheet

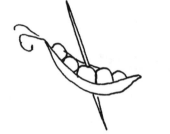

1) Put a small amount of each food on a piece of newspaper.

2) Use the eyedropper to put a drop of iodine on one food item at a time.

3) Watch what happens to each food, and record the results on the data sheet.

4) Decide whether or not the food contains starch, and mark your answers on the data sheet.

CAUTION:

Iodine is poison.
Handle with care.
Do not eat any of the foods!
Throw them away.

What's Happening?
Iodine is an indicator for starch. That means that when iodine and starch get together, they react to cause the iodine to turn dark brown or blackish blue. Starch is made by plants, so the tests will reveal starch in foods that come from plants only.

Investigation

Starch Search

Test each food with a drop of iodine.
Record the result.
Write "yes" or "no" to tell if it contains starch.

FOOD	RESULT	STARCH ✓
APPLE		
SALT		
CHEESE		
CHEERIOS®		
SALTINE CRACKER		
KETCHUP		
SAUSAGE		
FLOUR		
HAMBURGER		
OTHER		

Caution: Iodine is poison. Handle with care. Do _not_ eat any of these foods. _Throw them away!_

Investigation

The Spectacular, Trained Can

Make this amazing can that will obey your commands.

You need:
- coffee can with no ends
- 2 plastic lids that fit the can
- short piece of string
- heavy metal nut
- scissors
- long rubber band

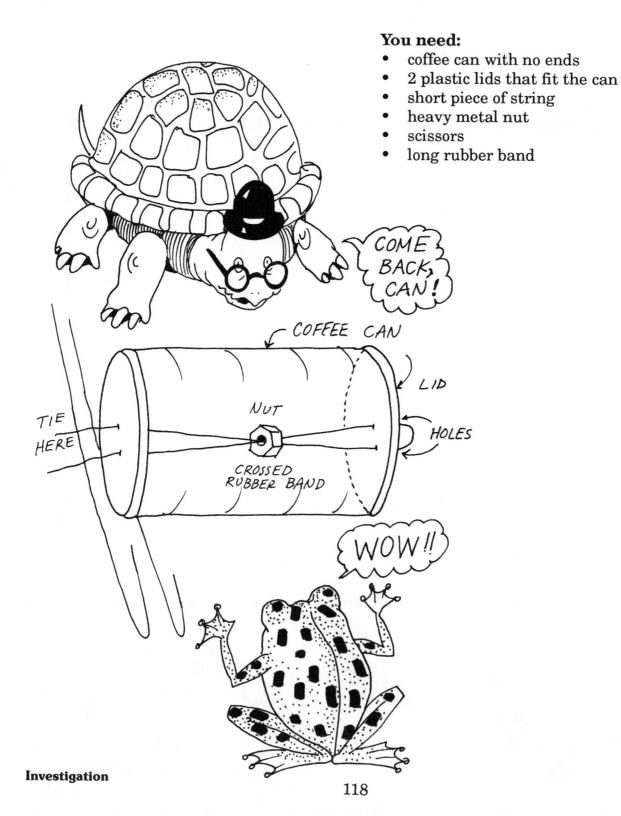

MAKE THE CAN

1) Punch two holes about 2 to 3 inches apart equally from the center of each plastic lid.

2) Cut the rubber band at one spot, and thread it through the holes on one lid. Put the lid on the can.

3) Cross the ends to form an "x" in the middle. Use the string to tie the nut to the center of the rubber band.

4) Thread the two ends through the holes in the other lid. Put the lid on, and tie the two ends in a knot outside the lid.

SHOW OFF THE TRAINED CAN

1) Roll the can away from you. Then say, "Can! Return to me!" The can will stop and come back to you.

2) Try rolling your can down a gently sloped hill, and demonstrate how it can even climb back up a hill to obey your command.

what a great trick!

What's Happening?
As the can rolls, the weight in the center causes the rubber band to twist and store energy. When it is twisted as tightly as possible, it has stored as much energy as it can, and it will stop. Then the rubber band starts untwisting and releasing the stored energy. This causes the can to roll back toward its starting place.

Investigation

Nonstop Spinner

Once you learn this trick, you can keep this button spinning for a long time, maybe forever!

You need:
- large button with 2 holes
- 3 feet of fine string

1) Thread the button onto the string as shown. Tie the ends of the string to make a large loop, and move the button to the center.

2) Hold one end of the loop in each hand. Twirl the button toward you until the string is very twisted.

3) Pull your hands apart to straighten the string. What happens? Now relax the string a bit. What happens?

4) Keep straightening and relaxing the string. Try doing this slowly and quickly. How does this affect the spinning? How long can you keep the button spinning?

What's Happening?
Twisting the string causes energy to be stored in it. When you straighten the string, the stored energy goes into the button, causing it to spin. The spinning button transfers energy to the string. When you relax and pull on the string again, you're adding more energy to the button. This energy transfer will continue to keep the button spinning for a long time. A little energy is lost with each transfer, so unless you keep adding energy by pushing and pulling the string, the spinning will eventually stop.

Investigation

Paper With Muscle

Would you believe a piece of paper is strong enough to hold a book? Try this and you'll be convinced.

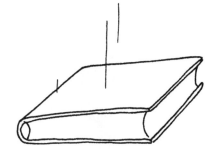

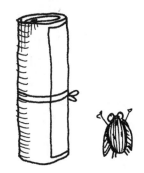

You need:
- several sheets of paper
- rubber bands
- scissors
- books of various sizes and weights
- 2 bricks

1) Roll a piece of paper into a tube. Put a rubber band around it. Stand the tube on end, and carefully lay a light book on it. Add another book. How many can it hold?

2) Try making paper tubes of different sizes, and test them to see how strong they are.

3) Fold another piece of paper into an accordian. Lay it across two bricks to make a bridge. Put bricks at both ends to keep the pleats in the accordian from spreading out. Lay a book on the bridge. How many books can it hold?

What's Happening?
A tube has much more strength than a flat object. As paper is wrapped around itself or folded, it gains strength.

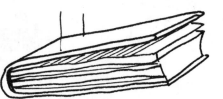

Investigation

The Force Is With You

When you perform these tricks, your friends will be surprised and impressed with your "special powers."

You need:
- 3 friends (including one bigger than you)
- 6" paper circle with target painted on it
- broom

TRICK # 1

1) Ask a bigger friend to hold both arms out straight and grab an upside-down broom.

2) Put one of your hands around the broom near its center, between the friend's hands.

3) Tell your friend to try and push you over by pushing against the broom. He must keep straight arms.

4) As the friend pushes toward you, push straight up on the broom with bent arms. You'll never lose!

What's Happening?
You have a special power called leverage. Your bent arm is a lever which helps with any work by allowing the weight to be moved with less effort. Straight arms don't have as much strength, so you can offset the force of the bigger friend's hard pushing with a much smaller force.

Investigation

TRICK # 2

1) Put the paper target on the floor.

2) Get three friends to hold the broom upside down near the bristle end. The handle should be off the ground at knee level or higher straight above the target.

3) Place the palm of your hand against the end of the broom handle.

4) Tell your friends to try and push the broom handle straight down and touch the target and that you all by yourself will keep them from doing it.

5) As they push down, you push sideways. They'll never be able to push the broom handle straight down!

What's Happening?
Two forces are at work here. You exert a sideways force, and they exert a downward force. Even though theirs is strong, it doesn't interfere with yours. Your small sideways force is enough to keep them from pushing the broom straight down.

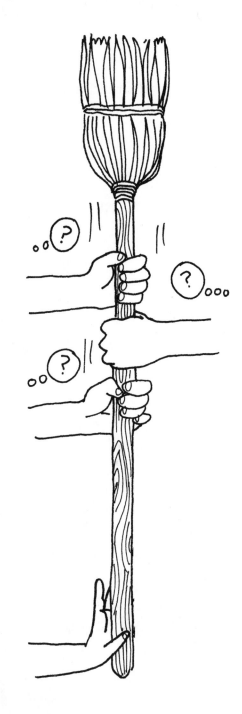

Investigation

Oh! For The Strength Of A Straw!

When you plunge a flimsy little straw through a hard raw potato, your friends will think you're the one with the muscle. But you don't have to tell them it's the potato that's the strong man.

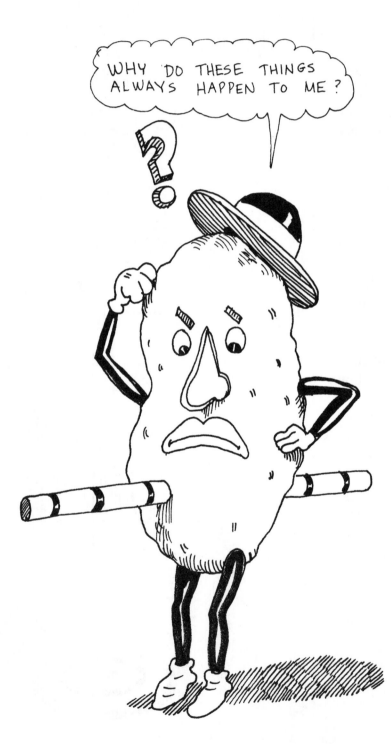

You need:
- several paper or plastic straws
- several fresh, thin-skinned baking potatoes
- water

1) Soak potatoes for five minutes, and wash them until they are clean. Dry them off.

2) Practice this trick: hold a straw tightly between your first finger and thumb at a right angle to the potato. Hold the potato in the other hand. Jab the straw hard into the potato. Make sure you're jabbing at a right angle. It should go right through the potato.

What's Happening?
When a force (a push or a pull) is applied along the entire length of the straw, it gives the straw unbelievable strength. Here's why: all the force of your push is concentrated on the small circle at the end of the straw. With so much force at that one spot, the straw is able to pierce the hard potato.

Another Strong Straw Trick

Is a straw strong enough to pick up a bottle? You bet!

You need:
- several straws
- a glass soft drink bottle

1) Bend a straw about 2 inches from the top.

2) Push the bent end of the straw into the bottle and wiggle it around until it is wedged between the two sides of the bottle.

3) Carefully pull on the straw, and the bottle should lift!

What's Happening?
The pull (a force) of the bottle's weight is distributed along the entire length of the straw. A force applied along such a length gives the straw the ability to hold a lot of weight. In addition, the weight of the bottle is pushing (another force) against the straw at the two points where the bent straw touches the bottle on the inside. Together these forces are stronger than the force exerted by the bottle's weight.

EX-STRAW-DINARY, ISN'T IT ?!?

125

Investigation

Miniboomerangs

You don't have to go to Australia to test a boomerang. You can make your own and try it out today without leaving town.

You need:
- tracing paper or thin typing paper
- lightweight cardboard
- colored markers
- scissors
- pencil

1) Trace this pattern and cut it out of thin cardboard.

2) Decorate it with markers.

3) Lay it on the first finger of your left hand. Hold it out in front of your body.

4) With your right hand, flick it with a quick snap of your index finger and knock it off. This will send it flying.

5) Watch where it goes.

What's Happening?
As the boomerang flies through the air, its two arms turn in opposite directions. This produces a force known as torque. Torque makes the shape tip to one side so that the boomerang rotates (twists) and returns to where it started.

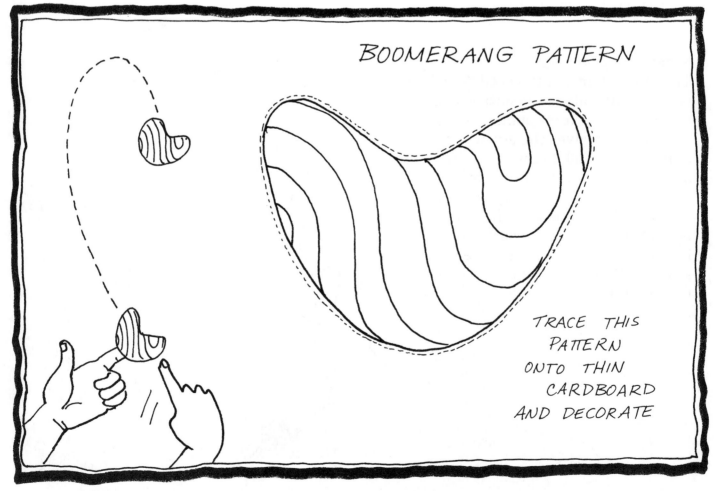

BOOMERANG PATTERN

TRACE THIS PATTERN ONTO THIN CARDBOARD AND DECORATE

Uptight Glasses

Try this trick to see how a little water makes it impossible to pull two glasses apart.

You need:
- 2 heavy plastic drinking glasses of the same size
- hot and cold water
- ice
- cooking pot

1) Put one glass inside the other.

2) Use your finger to spread water around the rim of the bottom glass so there is a thin layer of water between the two glasses.

3) Try to pull the glasses apart.

4) To get them apart, put some ice and cold water in the inside glass. Fill the pot with hot water, and dip the outer glass in hot water. Pull them apart immediately.

What's Happening?
Cohesion is a force which pulls the water molecules together. Another force, adhesion, is the tendency of water molecules to stick to the glass. In a very small space, these forces combine to work like glue. When you fill the inner glass with ice water, the cup contracts a bit. Hot water causes the outer glass to expand a bit. This allows you to break the forces and pull the glasses apart.

STUCK AGAIN! WHY DOES THAT ALWAYS HAPPEN?

Investigation

Eggs-actly What Is Inertia?

A force called inertia makes eggs and pennies do some strange things. Just watch!

DO YOU KNOW WHY THE EGG WOULDN'T CROSS THE FREEWAY?

HE WAS A LITTLE CHICKEN!

CLUCK CLUCK! CLUCK CLUCK

I LOVE FROGS

You'll need:
- glass
- playing card
- penny
- 1 uncooked egg
- 1 hard-boiled egg
- markers
- "An Eggs-citing Eggsperiment" data sheet

1) Place the card over the glass with the penny on top. Very quickly, pull the card straight off the glass. What happens to the penny?

2) Use markers to color the cooked egg. Then, spin each egg on its end. What happens?

3) Spin each egg on its side. Then try to stop them both with one touch of your finger. What happens?

What's Happening?
Inertia is the tendency of an object to resist moving if it's still or to resist changing the way it is moving. Inertia keeps the penny from moving with the card. Inertia in the boiled egg keeps the shell and the insides, which are both solid, moving at the same speed. But in the raw egg, the shell is solid and the inside is liquid. Inertia keeps both moving but at different rates, so the egg doesn't spin smoothly.

Investigation

An Eggs-citing Eggsperiment

The Penny Trick

Draw what happened to the penny.

Tell why._____

The Spinning Eggs

Draw what happened to the cooked egg

...to the uncooked egg.

What happened when you touched the cooked egg?

_____

_____

What happened when you touched the uncooked egg?

_____

_____

Data Sheet

Some Attractive Tricks

Gather a few magnets, and have fun trying these clever tricks with your friends.

You need:

- paper clips
- pennies
- hair pins
- bolts
- nuts
- Cheerios®
- cake pan
- glass of water
- thin plastic tray
- large needle
- markers

- ruler
- assortment of magnets
- plastic spoon
- straight pins
- safety pins
- nails
- buttons
- tiny sticks

- sand
- thumbtacks
- cookies
- cardboard
- poster board
- shoe box
- string
- glue

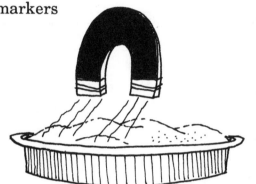

SAND SEARCH

Bury paper clips, pennies, hair pins, safety pins, a marker, needle, Cheerios®, plastic spoon, nails, nuts and bolts, sticks, buttons, thumbtacks, and straight pins in a cake pan full of sand. Pass a magnet over the sand.

What can you conclude? _____
_____

LIVE COOKIES

Stick a metal thumbtack in the bottom of several cookies. Lay them on a thin plastic tray. Hold a magnet under the tray and move it around. What happens to the cookies?

What can you conclude? _____
_____

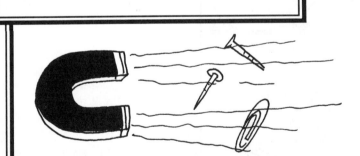

RECOVER THE CLIP

Drop a paper clip in a glass of water. Can you get it out with a magnet?

What can you conclude?
_____
_____

Investigation

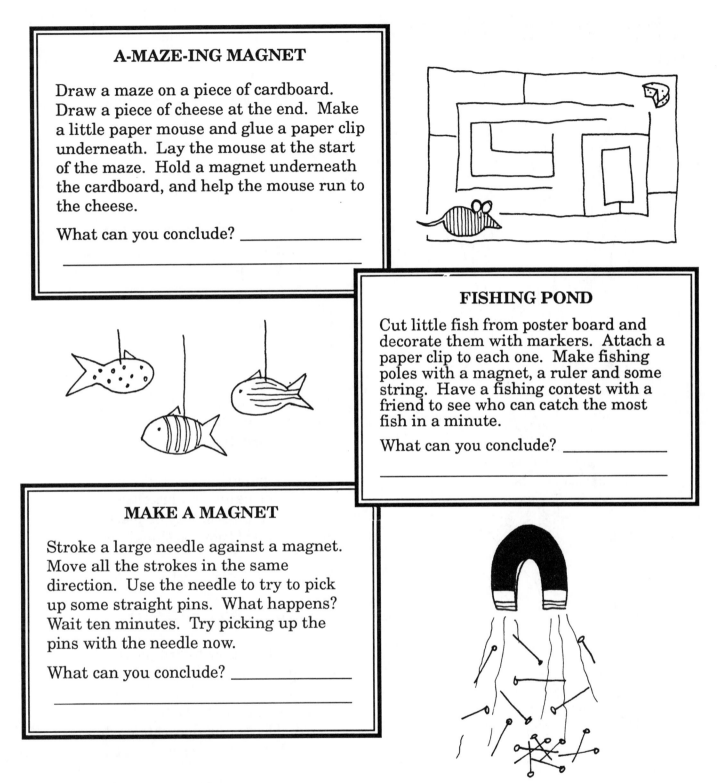

A-MAZE-ING MAGNET

Draw a maze on a piece of cardboard. Draw a piece of cheese at the end. Make a little paper mouse and glue a paper clip underneath. Lay the mouse at the start of the maze. Hold a magnet underneath the cardboard, and help the mouse run to the cheese.

What can you conclude? _____

_____

FISHING POND

Cut little fish from poster board and decorate them with markers. Attach a paper clip to each one. Make fishing poles with a magnet, a ruler and some string. Have a fishing contest with a friend to see who can catch the most fish in a minute.

What can you conclude? _____

_____

MAKE A MAGNET

Stroke a large needle against a magnet. Move all the strokes in the same direction. Use the needle to try to pick up some straight pins. What happens? Wait ten minutes. Try picking up the pins with the needle now.

What can you conclude? _____

_____

What's Happening?
Magnets attract many kinds of metal but not all. They do not attract non-metallic items. Also, magnetism will pass through some materials such as plastic and cardboard.

Investigation

Theater of Magnets

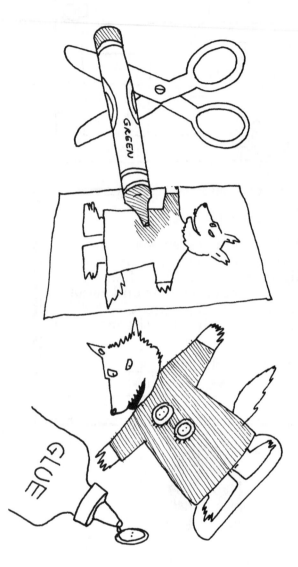

Magnets help you create an unusual puppet theater that will give you hours of fun.

You need:
- several small blocks of wood or matchboxes
- poster board
- markers
- yarn
- felt scraps
- scissors
- glue
- small nails
- cardboard boxes
- several magnets
- several yardsticks or rulers
- string
- drawing paper
- crayons or paint and brushes
- large, thin plastic tray or piece of cardboard (not too thick)

CREATE THE STORY

1) Decide on a story to dramatize. Choose one you know, or make one up.

2) Make the story characters from poster board. Dress and decorate each one with fabric scraps, crayons, etc.

3) Glue each character to a block of wood or matchbox.

4) Glue a nail to the bottom of each block or matchbox.

MAKE THE PROPS

1) Make the stage by piling up two stacks of books to hold a tray or piece of cardboard between them.

2) Make scenery on drawing paper backdrops. Tape or glue these inside cardboard boxes to set behind the stage.

3) Use string to tie magnets onto the ends of yardsticks.

PRESENT THE PLAY

1) Invite an audience.

2) Get behind the cardboard box backdrop.

3) Set the characters on stage and move them around by placing the magnet sticks underneath the stage. The magnets allow you to make the characters move without your being seen.

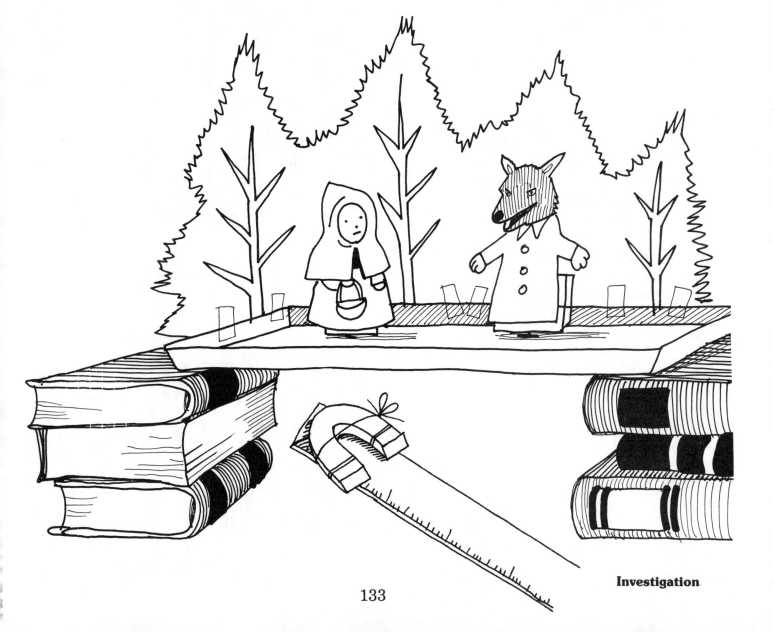

Investigation

The Wonderful, Magical Comb

You can turn an ordinary comb into a magic wand!

You need:
- a nylon or hard plastic comb
- tissue paper torn in tiny pieces
- table tennis ball
- blown-up balloon
- water faucet
- wool sock or scarf
- salt and pepper

1) Put tiny pieces of tissue paper on a table. "Charge" the comb by combing your hair vigorously twenty times. Then hold the comb over the pieces of paper. What happens?

2) Mix some salt and pepper on a tabletop. "Charge" the comb by combing your hair again or by rubbing it vigorously on the sock. Hold it over the salt and pepper. What happens?

3) Turn on cold water until you have a thin stream running. "Charge" your comb. Tilt it and hold it close to the water. What happens?

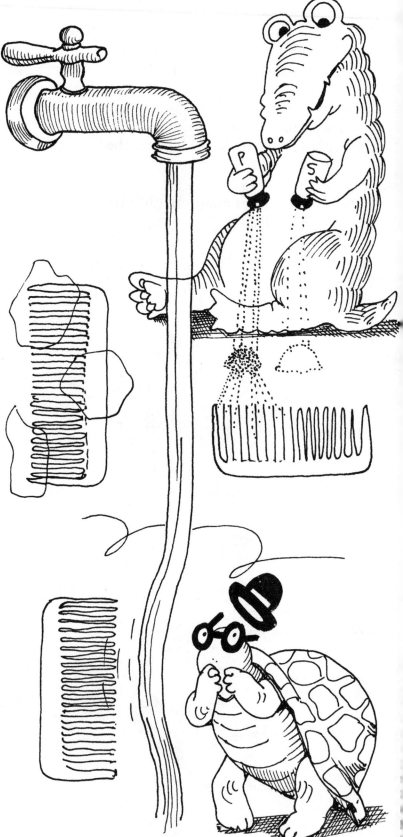

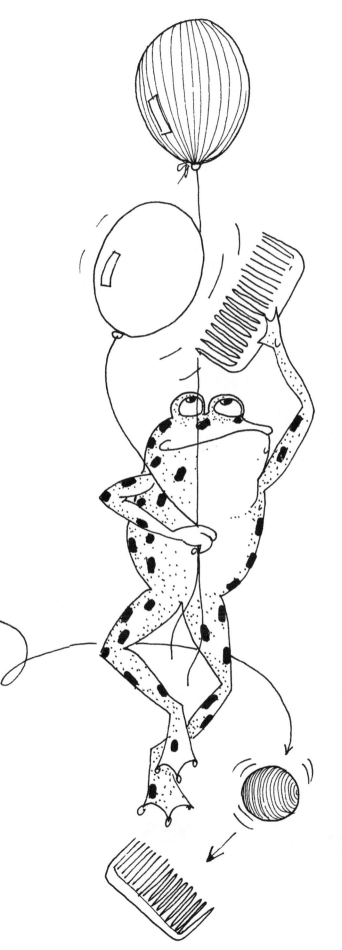

4) Don't "charge" the comb this time. Hold it close to the balloon. What happens? Can you explain why?

5) What do you think will happen if you "charge" the comb and hold it near the balloon? Try it.

6) "Charge" the comb and hold it about 1 inch from the table tennis ball. Pull the comb along slowly and watch what the ball does. What happens?

What's Happening?

When you rub the comb on your hair or the wool, it causes tiny particles called electrons to jump back and forth and leaves the comb (and your hair or sock) with an electrical charge called static electricity. Once an object is charged, it attracts other objects that have an opposite charge or no charge.

Investigation

Super Simple Circuit

Learn some things about electricity by making this quick and easy circuit of your own.

You need:
- adult helper
- small light bulb and socket
- large battery
- 2' long pieces of bell wire
- screwdriver
- small knife

1) Cut about 1 inch of plastic from each end of the wire. Twist the bare wires together to make the ends tight and neat.

2) Attach one piece of wire from the "+" terminal of the battery to one screw on the light socket.

3) Attach the second wire to the other screw on the light (leaving one end free).

4) Take the free end of the wire and touch it to the "-" terminal of the battery. What happens? Remove the wire from the "-" terminal. What happens? Make a hypothesis about what causes the light bulb to light.

What's Happening?
Electricity needs a complete path called a circuit in order to flow through the bulb. When you touch the wire to the battery, you close the circuit making a complete path. When you take the wire off, you break the circuit and electricity can't flow, even though the battery is attached by one wire to the light.

Lemon Power

Yes! It's true. You can make a battery from a lemon. Here's how to do it.

You need:
- brass thumbtack
- steel paper clip
- lemon
- flashlight bulb
- two 8" pieces of copper wire
- scissors

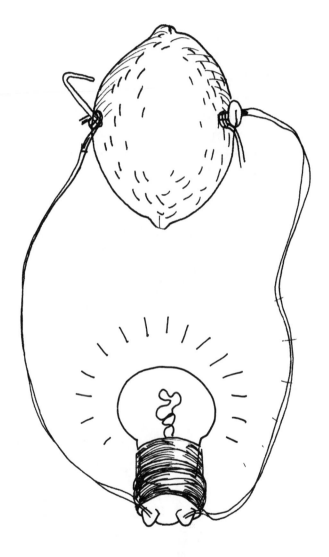

Make the battery:
1) Stick a paper clip in one side of the lemon and the tack into the other side.

2) Cut 1 inch of plastic from each end of the pieces of wire. Twist the bare ends of wire together neatly.

3) Attach one piece of wire to the paper clip and the other wire to the thumbtack.

See if it works:
Touch the two free wire ends to the two bumps on the bottom of the bulb. Does the bulb light?

What's Happening?
A battery has a liquid or paste chemical inside called an electrolyte that reacts to produce electricity. It also has electrodes, two different metal rods which carry electricity in and out of the battery. The lemon battery works because the lemon contains natural electrolytes, and the tack and paper clip function as electrodes.

Investigation

Add·A Switch

Electrical circuits become "fun" when you learn how to add switches that can turn the current on and off.

You need:
- adult helper
- 4 small bulbs and sockets
- paper clips
- good-sized battery
- 15' bell wire
- small blocks of wood
- scissors
- screwdriver
- metal thumbtacks
- "More Circuits, More Switches" data sheet

1) Make a circuit as shown with one 8 inch wire connecting a battery terminal and the bulb; a second wire attached to the bulb; and a third wire attached to the other battery terminal.

2) Make a switch by putting two thumbtacks into a block of wood a little more than 1 inch apart. Attach one free wire end to each tack. Put a paper clip around one of the tacks.

3) Touch the free end of the paper clip to the other tack. What happens to the light?

4) Use the diagrams on the data sheet to try more switches and bulbs in various arrangements. See which ones work to make the bulbs light.

What's Happening?
Closing the paper clip switch closes the circuit and allows the electricity to flow. Opening the switch stops the flow.

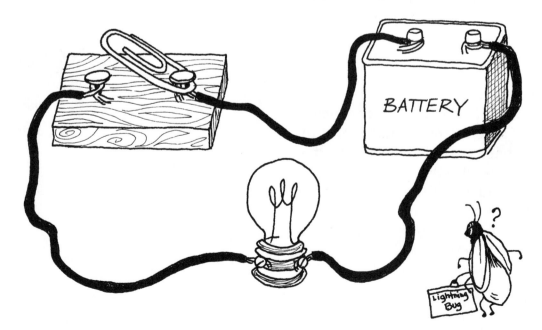

More Circuits, More Switches

········· WIRE
········· BATTERY
········· CONNECTED WIRES
········· SWITCH
········· BULB

Try each of these arrangements.
Tell what happens each time you close the switch.
Try to explain why.

Data Sheet

Light Tricks

These four investigations will let you "see" tricky and fascinating habits of light.

giggle
giggle

MYSTERIOUS BROKEN PENCIL

Put a pencil in a clear glass half full of water. Look straight at the pencil through the glass. Is it broken?

What's Happening?

You're seeing the top of the pencil just through the air and the glass and the bottom part through water. Light travels more slowly through water than through glass or air. Because of this, the light's direction changes a bit causing you to see the two parts of the pencil in different places.

You need:
- white paper
- pencil
- tape
- clear glass of water
- friend
- flashlight
- 2 long cardboard tubes (same size)
- large mirror
- 3 rectangular mirrors of same size
- colored cellophane or tissue paper

BACKWARD MESSAGES

Write a secret message backwards. Send it to a friend. Tell him to read it by holding it up to a mirror.

What's Happening?

Reflections are caused by light bouncing off things. When you see the reflected image of an object, your eyes see the object reversed.

WHAT'S YOUR ANGLE?

Lay two cardboard tubes on a table in front of a mirror. Make sure they touch the mirror at the same angle. Shine a flashlight in one tube. Have a friend look in the other tube to see the light coming right at him.

What's Happening?
When light hits an object at an angle (called the angle of incidence), it reflects back at the same angle (called the angle of reflection).

EASY KALEIDOSCOPE

Tape three mirrors together to form a tent shape. Cut a triangle from paper and tape it tightly to the end. Drop tiny scraps of colored cellophane or tissue into the center of the mirrors. Look in and see the patterns. Can you count the number of times the pattern is repeated?
Wiggle the scraps around to create new patterns.

What's Happening?
The patterns are made by repeated reflections in the mirrors. The paper reflects off the mirrors, and the mirrors reflect off each other. You should see each pattern repeated six times.

Investigation

141

Shadow Tricks

Try these escapades with shadows. You may be surprised at what you'll learn about light.

You need:
- black paper
- 4 flashlights
- a few friends
- crayons
- white chalk
- white bed sheet
- drinking straws
- glue
- large white mural paper

SHADOW SPOOK SHOW

Cut spooky shapes from black paper. Tape them onto straws. Hang a white sheet in an open doorway. Get some friends to watch from one side of the sheet while you get behind the sheet with a helper. As you hold the shapes and move them around, the helper shines one or two flashlights on the shapes to make the spook show.

SHADOW SHRINK

Get a friend to make a puppet with his hand and hold it up in front of a white wall. Shine a flashlight on the hand holding it close to the hand. Look at the shadow.
Then move the flashlight back away from the hand, and watch the shadow shrink.

Investigation

142

Shadow Chase

On a sunny day, play a game of
chase with your shadow.
See if you can step on it.
Try to get away from it.
Try to catch someone else's shadow.
Get together with some friends and
form a group shadow.

Double Shadow

In a slightly dark room, have two
people shine bright flashlights on you
from two different directions. How
many shadows do you have? How are
they different? Try this with three or
four flashlights.

Capture A Shadow

Have a friend draw around your
shadow on a piece of white mural
paper some sunny day. Or, sit still
in front of a piece of white paper
and have someone shine a bright
light at your head. Your shadow
can be traced around to capture a
silhouette of your head. Cut this
out of black and white paper at the
same time, and you'll have two
shadows.

What's Happening?

A shadow is made when the path of
light is blocked by something that light
will not pass through (something
opaque). The shadow is cast on the
opposite side from the light source. So
if there is more than one light source,
there will be multiple shadows.
When an object is close to the light
source, it blocks more light and makes
a larger shadow. As the light gets
further away, the object blocks less
light and the shadow shrinks.

Investigation

Rainbows In A Hurry

Here are five different ways to make a rainbow without waiting for one to appear by itself on a rainy day.

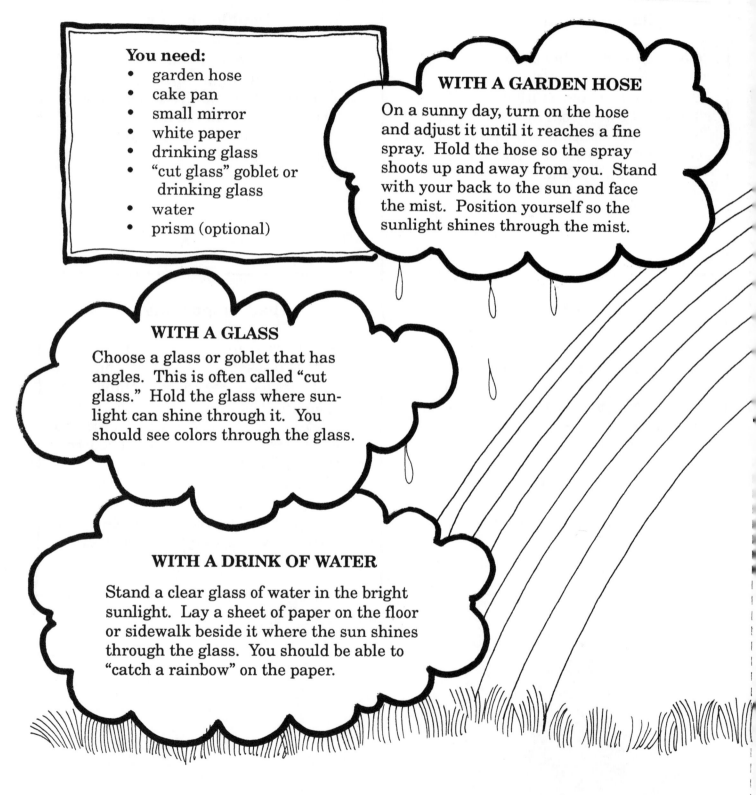

You need:
- garden hose
- cake pan
- small mirror
- white paper
- drinking glass
- "cut glass" goblet or drinking glass
- water
- prism (optional)

WITH A GARDEN HOSE

On a sunny day, turn on the hose and adjust it until it reaches a fine spray. Hold the hose so the spray shoots up and away from you. Stand with your back to the sun and face the mist. Position yourself so the sunlight shines through the mist.

WITH A GLASS

Choose a glass or goblet that has angles. This is often called "cut glass." Hold the glass where sunlight can shine through it. You should see colors through the glass.

WITH A DRINK OF WATER

Stand a clear glass of water in the bright sunlight. Lay a sheet of paper on the floor or sidewalk beside it where the sun shines through the glass. You should be able to "catch a rainbow" on the paper.

Investigation

WITH A MIRROR

Put a pan or tray of water in the bright sunlight. Set a mirror in the pan resting on its edge so the sun shines into the mirror. Hold a sheet of white paper very still to catch the reflection of the sun off the mirror.

WITH A PRISM

The most sure way to see a rainbow is to use a prism, a tent-shaped piece of glass with just the right angles for making rainbows. If you can use one, hold it so the sunlight can pass through it, and enjoy the colors.

What's Happening?

Sunlight appears to be white, but it consists up of various colors (called the spectrum). When light goes through water or glass at a slant, the rays of light are bent. The colors in the light each bend a little differently, so they come out of the glass or water at slightly different places. This separates them so you can see them; this causes a rainbow. The colors always "bend" the same amount, so they come out in the same order.

Investigation

Disappearing Colors

Try this trick to turn bright colors into white.

You need:
- 5" plate
- pencil
- scissors
- stiff cardboard
- paint in rainbow colors
- paintbrushes
- 3' of heavy string
- ruler

1) Draw around the plate and cut out a circle. Dot the center.

2) Poke two holes in the circle, each about 1 inch from the center.

3) Divide the circle into seven pie pieces, and paint each section one of the colors of the rainbow in the order shown.

4) When the paint is dry, thread the string through the holes and tie a knot to make a large loop.

5) Hold the loop around your fingers and turn the circle until the string is very twisted.

6) Make the circle spin by pulling your hands apart then closer together to alternately tighten and loosen the string. Watch what happens to the colors.

What's Happening?
White light is a combination of the colors of the spectrum. When the circle spins fast, your eyes mix the colors together and see white.

Investigation

146

What To Wear?

You can learn some things about light, heat, and color just by changing shirts on a sunny day.

You need:
- white shirt
- black or navy shirt
- black and white paper
- 2 paper cups
- tape
- scissors
- a sunny day
- ice cubes
- thermometer

1) Put on a white shirt and stand outside in the sun for five minutes. Put on a dark shirt and do the same. Do you notice any difference in how cool or warm you feel?

2) Wrap black paper around a paper cup. Wrap white paper around the other. Fill both with ice cubes and set them in the sun. Come back in 30 minutes and see which ice has melted more.

3) Wrap another cup with black paper and another with white. Fill both half full with water of the same temperature. Set them in the sun. Come back in an hour and measure the temperature of both glasses of water. Are they the same?

What's Happening?
Light colors reflect light and its heat away. Dark colors absorb light and change it into heat.

Investigation

147

Some Sound Ideas

Rulers, rocks, rubber bands, and such can help you learn how sounds are made and how you hear them.

You need:

- 2 glasses (same size)
- large rubber bands
- drinking straws
- heavy book
- cooking pot with lid
- aluminum foil
- sturdy plastic wrap
- water
- ruler
- pencil
- metal spoon
- string
- coffee can
- dry rice

FLAPPING RULER

Put a book near the edge of a table. Trap one end of a ruler under the book firmly by holding the book down with your hand. Bend the ruler up and let it go. Listen. What do you hear? What do you see?

SHAKING RUBBER BANDS

Stretch a large, thick rubber band across a cooking pot. Pluck it. What do you see? What do you hear?

QUIVERING BALL

Fill a glass half full of water. Make a ball of foil and hang it from a string so that it barely touches the glass. Bang on the glass with a metal spoon. What do you hear? Watch the foil ball. What happens to it?

WOBBLING THROAT

Touch your hand to your throat while you hum a favorite melody. What do you feel?

WIGGLING DRUM

Make a drum by fastening a circle of sturdy plastic wrap over the top of an empty coffee can with a rubber band. Lay some dry rice on top of the drum. Bang on the side of the drum. What happens to the rice?

SHIVERING LID

Hang a cooking pot lid from a string. Don't touch the string. Bang the lid with a metal spoon. What do you hear? What do you see?

What's Happening?

When you pluck the rubber band, bend the ruler and let go, or bang the pot lid. These objects start shaking slightly (vibrating). The vibrations cause the molecules in the air to start vibrating. These moving air molecules make other air molecules vibrate, and the chain reaction continues all the way to your ear where the moving air causes your eardrum to vibrate. This causes you to hear a sound. The sound of you humming is made by vibrations, also.

La la la la la

Clank Clank

Ping ... Ping

COFF

Investigation

149

More Strange Sounds

Try these tricks with sound.

You need:
- 2 metal spoons
- 2 plastic cups
- tub or sink of water
- friend
- string
- scissors
- fork

SINGING SPOONS

Tie a spoon in the center of a 3 foot piece of string. Hold the ends of the string in your ears while someone bangs on the spoon with another spoon. What do you hear?

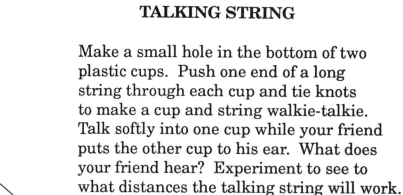

TALKING STRING

Make a small hole in the bottom of two plastic cups. Push one end of a long string through each cup and tie knots to make a cup and string walkie-talkie. Talk softly into one cup while your friend puts the other cup to his ear. What does your friend hear? Experiment to see to what distances the talking string will work.

Investigation

HEARING TEETH

Bang a fork with a spoon. When the sound begins to fade, touch the handle of the fork to your teeth. What do you hear?

CLANGING ROCKS

Knock two rocks together. Do this again under water in a sink or bathtub. Your ear must be under the water, too. How has the sound of the banging rocks changed?

What's Happening?
Sound vibrations travel through solids and liquids faster and better than they do through air. Your teeth, the water in the tub, the string, the spoons, and fork all carry the sound waves well so you hear the sounds more loudly than you do through just plain air.

Long ago, Indians listened to the ground to find out if anyone was approaching on horses. The vibrations caused by the horses hooves traveled through the solid ground and could be heard there before they could be heard through the air.

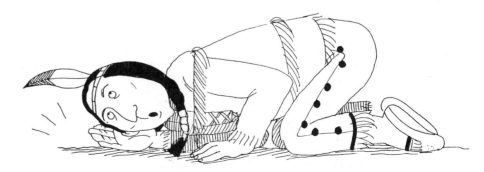

Investigation

151

What Makes The Pitch?

A pitch is not just something you find in a baseball game.
It also shows up in sounds and music; it tells you how high or low a note is.

You need:
- 8 glass bottles (same size)
- water
- metal spoons
- a flat block of wood
- nails
- hammer
- fishing line
- string
- pot lids of different sizes
- "Pitch Switch" data sheet

1) Put a different amount of water in each bottle.

2) Hang the pot lids from strings in a place where they can swing free.

3) Make a simple harp by hammering pairs of nails at different distances on the wood block. Tightly string fishing line between each pair of nails.

4) Follow the instructions on the data sheet to investigate how different pitches are made.

What's Happening?
Pitch (the highness or lowness) of a sound depends on the number (frequency) of vibrations. Faster vibrations produce high sounds, slower vibrations produce low sounds. Short strings, smaller lids, and less air in the bottle all cause higher pitches because the smaller things vibrate faster than something longer or bigger.

Investigation

Pitch Switch

Bang on each of the bottles with a spoon.

Line them up in order of pitch from lowest to highest sound.

Which bottle has the lowest pitch? _____

Which has the highest? _____

What can you conclude about pitch? _____

_____

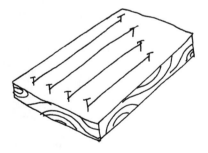

Bang on the pot lids with a spoon.

Which has the lowest pitch? _____

Which has the highest pitch? _____

What can you conclude about pitch?

_____

_____

Pluck on the fishing line strings of your harp.

Which makes the highest sound? _____

Which makes the lowest? _____

What can you conclude about pitch? _____

_____

What can you say about how pitch is made?

_____

153

Data Sheet

Music Makers

Have a good time making wonderful sounds with your own homemade orchestra. All these instruments can be made in minutes.

You need:
- drinking glasses
- water
- hanger
- metal pail
- ruler
- wooden blocks
- pot lids
- rubber bands
- lots of friends
- silverware
- dry rice
- glass bottles
- string
- broomstick
- sandpaper
- salt box
- cooking pots
- shoe box

- Fill glasses to different levels with water. Bang on them with a spoon to produce different notes.

- String some silverware on a hanger. Use a spoon to bang on your "dinnerware chimes."

- Cover two wooden blocks with sandpaper. Rub them together to produce an interesting grating sound.

- Get a big metal tub or pail. Stand or tape a wooden broomstick to it. Fasten a string tightly from the stick to the bottom of the pail. Pluck the string, and you have a bass fiddle!

- Bang two pot lids together. They make great cymbals. Try lids of different sizes.

- Get an assortment of bottles to blow in. You'll get different sounds from different sizes. You can add water to some of them to change the pitch.

- Bang on different sizes of cooking pots.

- Bend and flap a wooden ruler for an eerie sound.

- Fill a salt box with dry rice for a shaker that adds to your rhythm section.

- Make a rubber band harp by stretching rubber bands over an open shoe box. Pluck the rubber bands. For different notes, try boxes of different sizes.

Investigation

Heat Wave

A simple pinwheel can teach you something about one way that heat travels.

You need:
- lightweight cardboard circle
- markers
- thumbtack
- scissors
- wooden dowel
- ruler
- pencil
- lamp, radiator, or other heating unit

1) Decorate the circle with markers.

2) Using a pencil and ruler, divide it into six sections. Number them as shown.

3) Cut each line as shown, not quite to the center, and bend the numbered corners toward the center.

4) Push the thumbtack through all the corners, and pin the wheel to the wooden stick.

5) Hold it above a heat source such as a lamp or a heater (not one that blows air), and watch what happens to the pinwheel.

What's Happening?
When air is heated, it expands and the molecules move further apart. This makes the warm air lighter, so it rises as cooler, heavier air sinks. The movement of the air sets up currents which move the pinwheel. This air movement is called convection.

Earth & Space Sciences

You Can't See It, But It's There

Things that look empty often are full of air. You can't see it, but air is there. It can do all sorts of things. Try these experiments to learn some things about air.

You need:
- 3 balloons of the same size
- index cards
- 5 sheets of thin paper
- cereal bowl
- clear drinking glass
- thin wooden dowel
- string
- plastic bag
- book
- water

1) Blow up a balloon, but don't tie it shut. Let it go. How can you tell there was air in the balloon?

2) Fill half the bowl full of water. Turn the glass upside down and set it directly down in the water. Do not tip the glass.

   Does the water go into the glass? What is in the glass? What do you think will happen if you tip the glass sideways? Try it. What happens? Why?

3) Lay several pieces of paper on the floor. Drop a book near them. What happens to the paper? What made that happen?

Investigation

4) Open a plastic bag and pull it through the air to "catch" some air. Fasten it tightly. Squeeze and feel the bag. Can you "feel" the air?

5) Drop an index card straight down (Picture 1). Then drop one with the flat side pointed down (Picture 2). What is the air doing to the second card?

6) Make a balance with two blown-up balloons the same size. The balloons should balance. Then pop one balloon. What does this convince you about air?

Investigation

Just A Lot Of Hot Air

Some surprising things happen when air gets heated!

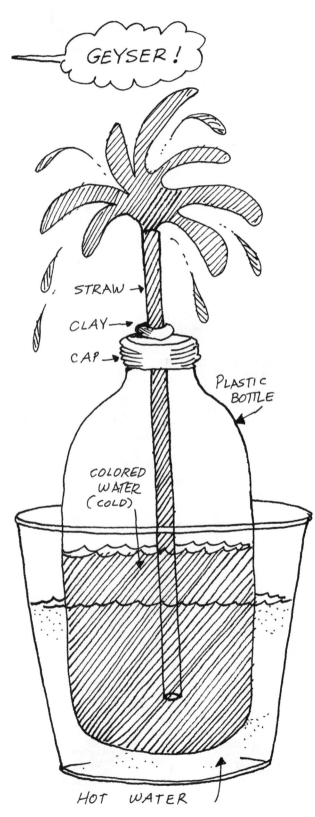

GEYSER !

STRAW →

CLAY →

CAP →

PLASTIC
BOTTLE

COLORED
WATER
(COLD)

HOT WATER

You need:
- plastic bottle with screw-on top
- glass bottle (no top necessary)
- food coloring
- plastic straw
- plastic-based clay
- good sized, stretchy balloon
- scissors
- bucket or large tall bowl
- very hot water
- cold water

HOT AIR TRICK # 1

1) Fill the plastic bottle half full of cold water. Add food coloring.

2) Poke a hole in the bottle cap with scissors. Push the straw into the hole, and seal off the space around the straw well with a hunk of clay.

3) Set the bottle in the bucket. Pour very hot tap water into the bucket to the level of the top of the bottle.

4) Wait and watch. What happens? Can you explain why?

What's Happening?
Hot water warms the air in the bottle. As air warms, it expands and puts pressure on the water in the bottle. This pressure forces the water up the straw.

Investigation

160

HOT AIR TRICK # 2

1) Fill the bucket with very cold water.

2) Fill the glass bottle with very hot tap water.

3) Dump the hot water out of the bottle, and immediately stretch the balloon tightly over the neck of the bottle.

4) What happens? Can you explain why?

5) Now set the bottle into the bucket of cold water.

6) What happens? Can you explain why?

What's Happening?

When you warmed the bottle with hot water, the bottle made the air inside warm. Warm air expands (or takes up more space), so the air pushed out into the balloon. The cold water caused the air in the bottle to cool down and contract. Then the air in the bottle took up less space, and air pressure outside the bottle pushed the balloon down into the bottle.

Investigation

Air Plays Tricks On You

See if you can figure out how the air around you keeps you from succeeding at these simple tasks.

You need:
- ruler
- large balloon
- plastic bottle with screw-on top
- "What's Air Up To?" data sheet
- newspaper
- scissors
- dishpan
- water
- large glass bottle

Lift A Newspaper
Lay a ruler on the table with about half of it over the edge. Cover the rest of the ruler with the newspaper. With your fist, hit the free end of the ruler sharply and quickly to lift the paper.

Drain Water Out Of A Hole
Poke a small hole in the side of the plastic bottle near the bottom. Hold your finger over it. Fill the bottle to the very top with water. Screw the top on tightly. Hold the bottle over the dishpan and take your finger off the hole.

Blow Up A Balloon
Put the balloon into the glass bottle and stretch the end of the balloon over the bottle's neck. Blow it up.

What's Happening?
1) Air pressure on the newspaper holds it down when the ruler is hit suddenly.
2) Air pressure coming through the hole in the plastic bottle is stronger than gravity, and there's no pressure on top of the water, so water stays in the bottle. Also, surface tension holds water together across the small hole.
3) You cannot blow up the balloon in the glass bottle because the bottle is full of air. When you blow into the balloon, the air in the bottle is compressed, and compressed air exerts more pressure on the balloon than you can blow into it.

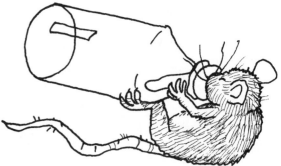

Investigation

What's Air Up To?

Newspaper Lift

What happened?_____

_____

Can you explain why? _____

_____

Now hit the ruler slowly. Does this change

the results? _____

Why? _____

_____

Hole In The Bottle

Did water drain out? _____

Why?_____

_____

Unscrew the cap. What happens?

_____

Why?_____

_____

The Balloon

What happened?_____

_____

Why? _____

_____

163

Can't Stand The Pressure?

Air can squish a bottle, squash a can, hold water in an upside-down glass, and make it impossible for you to drink a can or bottle of juice. Here's proof!

You need:
- 2-liter plastic soda bottle with a lid
- gallon metal can with a lid
- boiling and cold water
- piece of sturdy, flat cardboard
- drinking glass
- can of juice
- bottle of juice
- can opener
- straws
- modeling clay

The Squished Bottle
Pour about 2 inches of hot water into the plastic bottle. Let steam rise out of the top, then quickly screw the lid on tightly. Watch what happens.

The Squashed Can
Pour 1/2 cup of boiling water into the can until steam rises out the top. Immediately screw on the top tightly. Watch the can carefully. What happens?

What's Happening?
Air pressure is what "squashes" them. The heat from the hot water caused the air to expand. When the air cooled, it contracted, resulting in less pressure inside the bottle and can than outside. The greater pressure outside pushed on the can and bottle and caused them to collapse.

The Upside-Down Glass That Won't Spill

1) Fill a drinking glass to the very top with water. The water should spill over the top a bit.
2) Carefully lay the cardboard square to completely cover the top of the glass. Holding the cardboard on top, turn the glass over until it is straight upside down. Stop holding the cardboard on. It will stay on by itself.

The Undrinkable Drinks

1) Use the can opener to make a small hole in a can of juice. Try to drink the juice. What happens when you punch another hole in the can?

2) Open a bottle of juice. Add enough water to fill the bottle to the very top. Put in a straw. Use clay to completely block the opening of the bottle around the straw. Try to drink the juice.

What's Happening?

There is no air in the glass of water to push down on the cardboard. The air pressure pushing up on the cardboard is greater than the weight of the water. And the juice won't come out of the hole unless air can get in to push down on it; you need a second hole to let air in. Juice won't go up the straw because no air is getting in to push down on the juice.

Investigation

The Famous Egg-In-The-Bottle Trick

Learn how to make an egg go magically into a bottle with a mouth smaller than the egg. What's more, you can get the egg out, too!

You need:

- glass baby bottle
- several eggs slightly larger than the mouth of the bottle, hard-boiled and shelled
- cooking oil
- matches
- 5 inch squares of paper
- water

Can't be done!

Getting The Egg In

1) Grease the mouth of the bottle with oil.

2) Fold one square of paper accordian-style. Light it with a match, and drop it in the bottle.

3) Right away, set the egg in the bottle's mouth.

4) The egg will gradually drop.

What's Happening?

The burning paper produces gases in the bottle. Some of them leak out. The rest cool when the flame goes out. As they cool, the gases contract leaving a partial vacuum in the bottle. The air pressure outside the bottle is then stronger than the pressure inside. So the egg is pushed in by the air!

IT CAN BE DONE!

Getting The Egg Out

1) Fill the bottle with water to rinse out the burned paper. You'll have to hold the egg out of the way with your finger.

2) Hold the bottle upside down. Blow into the bottle past the egg as hard as you can. Keep the bottle upside down so the egg blocks the opening.

3) The egg should drop right into your hand.

What's Happening?
Blowing forced extra air into the bottle. The egg kept it in. The pressure of the air behind the egg is greater than the pressure outside the bottle, and it pushes the egg out.

167

Investigation

Disappearing Water

After the rain stops, a puddle starts to disappear. Where does the water go?

You need:
- 4 jars the same size (one with a lid)
- permanent marker
- water

1) Fill four jars almost full of water. All jars must have exactly the same amount. Use a marker to draw a line showing the level of the water in each jar.

2) Put a top on one jar. Place it in a spot that is not too cool or too warm. Put a jar next to it. Then place another jar in a warm spot and the last jar in a cool spot.

3) Every day, mark the water level in each jar. After five days compare the jars. Where has the water gone? Why do you think the levels are different?

What's Happening?
The water doesn't disappear. Moving molecules at the surface of the water get bumped by surrounding molecules in the air. This is called evaporation. Water evaporates faster in a warm spot.

Brrrr....

Reappearing Water

You can make water magically appear. You can make it rain!

Cookie Sheet

Melting Ice Cubes

Tea Kettle

Hot Plate

You need:
- teakettle full of water
- hot plate
- bowl of ice cubes
- cookie sheet
- several books or bricks

1) Set up your experiment to look like this.

2) Plug in the hot plate. Then watch what happens when the steam from the boiling water hits the cold tray of ice. Where do you think the rain comes from?

What's Happening?
The cloud you see above the teakettle is tiny drops of water in the air, water vapor. The cold tray cools the air. Cool air can't hold as much water, so the water drops. This process is called condensation.

Never touch steam or hot water vapor. It will burn you!

169   **Investigation**

You're All Wet!

You can learn a lot about science with wet feet. Get your socks wet and find out why wet feet can keep you cool.

You need:
- 5 pairs cotton socks (all the same kind)
- a sunny, breezy day
- clock
- water
- "Got Wet Feet?" data sheet

1) Put on one dry sock. Wet another sock, wring it out, and put it on. Go outside. How does each foot feel?

2) While you're outside, wet one arm. How does it feel?

3) Wet and wring nine more socks.
   - Wad one up and leave it inside.
   - Inside, lay one flat and hang one.
   - Hang two out in the sun - one where it's breezy, one where it's still.
   - Hang two in the shade - one where it's breezy, one where it's still.
   - Lay one flat in the sun; lay one flat in the shade.

4) Get out your clock, and find out how much time it takes each sock to dry. Record the results on your data sheet.

What's Happening?
The wet foot is cool because the water is evaporating. When water evaporates it turns into a gas (water vapor). Heat is needed for water to evaporate, and some of the heat comes from your body. So your body feels cooler. Evaporation happens faster, then, in places that are warm. Moving air helps water evaporate faster, too.

Investigation

170

Got Wet Feet?

How does the foot with the wet sock feel in comparison to the foot with the dry

sock? _____

_____

Tell about the temperature of the wet arm. _____

_____

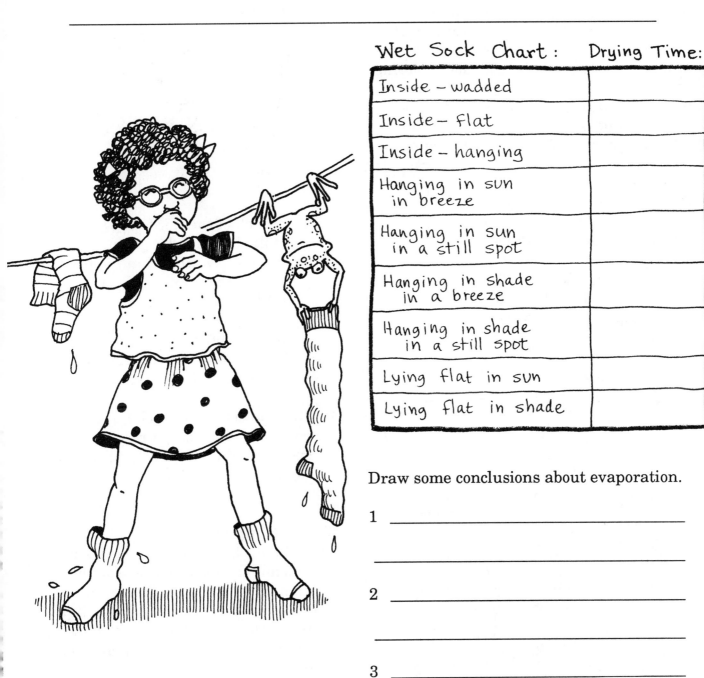

Wet Sock Chart:	Drying Time:
Inside – wadded	
Inside – flat	
Inside – hanging	
Hanging in sun in breeze	
Hanging in sun in a still spot	
Hanging in shade in a breeze	
Hanging in shade in a still spot	
Lying flat in sun	
Lying flat in shade	

Draw some conclusions about evaporation.

1 _____

_____

2 _____

_____

3 _____

Data Sheet

The Floating Egg

If you think an egg won't float in water, think again. Here's a way to surprise your friends by showing them that you can make it happen.

You need:

- uncooked egg
- pitcher
- soft drink
- molasses
- orange juice
- salt
- measuring cups
- tall, clear glass
- "Density Surprises" data sheet
- widemouth jar
- water
- cooking oil
- syrup
- food coloring
- tablespoon
- milk
- motor oil
- lots of news-papers

1) Pour 2 cups of water into the jar. Gently set the egg on the water.

2) Remove the egg and mix 6 table-spoons of salt into the water. Put in the egg. What happens this time?

3) Pour each of these into the glass carefully in the order given. Do not mix. Watch what happens.
   1/2 cup motor oil
   1/2 cup cooking oil
   1/2 cup syrup
   1/2 cup soft drink
   1/4 cup milk mixed with blue food coloring

4) Test the density of each liquid on the data sheet by dropping a spoonful of it carefully onto water. Record your results.

What's Happening?
Some liquids are more dense than others. This means the molecules are closer together than in water. Things will float more easily on dense liquids. If a liquid floats on water, it is less dense than water. If it sinks, it is more dense than water.

172

Investigation

Density Surprises

1. Draw what happens to the egg in plain water.

2. Draw what happens to the egg in salt water.

3. Can you hypothesize why it is easier to float in the ocean than in a lake?

4. Are these things below more or less dense than water?
Drop a spoonful of each on water. Check one column to show your conclusion.

	LESS DENSE THAN WATER	MORE DENSE THAN WATER
MOLASSES		
SODA POP		
COOKING OIL		
MOTOR OIL		
MILK		
SYRUP		

5. Draw the glass of layered liquids. Label each liquid.

6. Which is more dense:

cooking oil or motor oil? _____

molasses or syrup? _____

cooking oil or syrup ? _____

milk or syrup? _____

Investigation

Water Is Pushy

Why do some things sink and others float? See if you can figure out which things will float and why.

You need:
- deep pan or bucket of water
- towel
- salt
- plastic-based clay
- "Sinkers Or Floaters?" data sheet
- items listed on the data sheet

1) Form two clay balls about 2 inches in diameter. Shape one of them into as large a boat as you can.

2) Lay the boat and the ball on the water. Do they float?

3) Try holding a table tennis ball under the water. Let go of it under water. What happens?

4) Make a guess about each item on the data sheet. Then test to see if it sinks or floats.

5) Stir 2 cups of salt into the water, and repeat the tests. What do you find out?

What's Happening?
When you put an object in water, it pushes some of the water away. This is called displacement. The more water that is displaced, the harder the water pushes back. An object floats if it displaces more water than its own weight. The clay in the shape of the boat displaced more water than its weight, but the ball of clay did not. The table tennis ball floated for the same reason. Salt water pushes back harder on objects than plain water, so things float more easily in salt water.

Investigation

174

Sinkers or Floaters?

Write "S" for sink and "F" for float.

	My Guess	Test	In Salt Water
aluminum foil square			
aluminum foil ball			
table tennis ball			
wood pencil			
pen			
paper clip			
washcloth			
soap bar			
glass jar			
glass jar with lid			
orange			
dry sponge			
wet sponge			
paper cup			
block of wood			
cork			
marble			
empty can with plastic lid			
can of soup			
modeling clay ball			
modeling clay boat			
eraser			
5g sodium metal			

Data Sheet

Water's Invisible Skin

Did you ever notice that water has skin? Here are some amazing tricks that water can do with the help of its invisible skin.

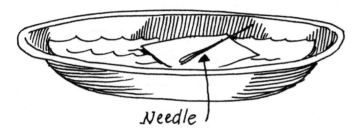

Needle

You need:
- facial tissue
- needle
- water
- 4 shallow dishes
- plastic berry basket
- baby powder
- drinking glass
- 25 pennies
- drawing paper
- scissors
- liquid detergent

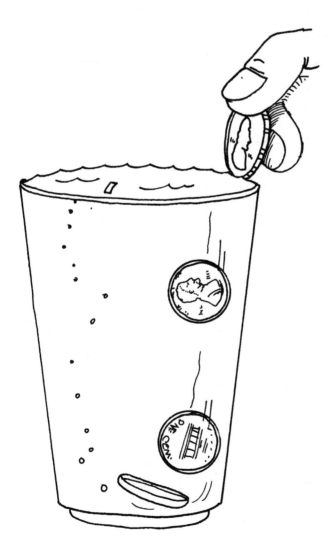

1) Put some water in a dish. Cut a square of facial tissue a little larger than the needle. Gently lay the facial tissue on top of the water, and set the needle on it. Watch what happens.

2) Fill a glass to the very top with water, but do not let it spill over. Very carefully, slide a penny just over the edge so it slips down the side into the water. Keep adding pennies, and watch the water rise above the glass. How many pennies can you add before the water spills?

What's Happening?
The molecules in water really stick together. Their strong attraction for each other holds the water and appears to give it a skin. This is called surface tension. The tension is strong enough to hold the needle and to hold the molecules together even when the water is a little above the rim of the glass.

3) Fill a dish half full of water. Set a plastic berry basket gently on the surface. The surface tension will keep it from sinking. Squeeze 1 drop of liquid detergent into the water. What happens?

4) Pour water in a clean dish. Make sure there is no soap film in the dish. Sprinkle baby powder on the surface. Drop a small bit of detergent in one side of the dish. What happens?

5) Cut out a paper boat leaving a slot in the back that has a small hole. Place this in a dish of clean water. Squeeze a drop of detergent into the hole in the slot. Watch what happens.

What's Happening?
The detergent breaks the surface tension. This causes the basket to sink. The change in the tension also causes the powder and the boat to move to the other side of the dish where the tension is greater.

Investigation

Bubble Mania

Mix together a big batch of bubble soup, gather a bunch of friends, and have a good time learning about science while you blow bubbles.

BUBBLE SOUP

- 1 cup liquid dish-washing detergent
- 3 cups water
- 1 cup glycerine

* Chill overnight

You need:
- Bubble Soup
- large, flat pan
- cardboard tubes
- wax paper cups
- wire coat hangers
- newspapers
- scissors
- plastic straws
- cotton string
- thin wire

GIANT BUBBLES

1) Pour a batch of bubble soup into a flat pan.

2) Shape the coat hanger into a circle and dip it in the soup.

3) Practice blowing gently to make gigantic bubbles. Or, try waving the wire circle gently through the air.

TABLE BUBBLES

1) Pour some bubble soup on the table.
2) Try blowing on the soup with straws or cardboard tubes.

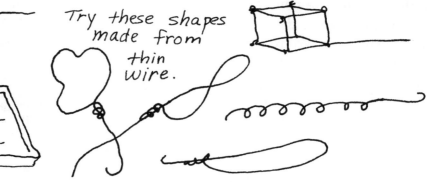

Try these shapes made from thin wire.

BUBBLES ON THE RUN

1) Thread a piece of 3 foot string through two straws as shown, and tie the two ends in a knot.
2) Dip this into the bubble soup.
3) To release the bubble, touch the two straws together gently, or run holding the straw-string bubblemaker in the air.

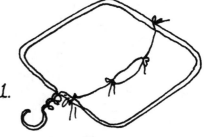

SOAP FILM BUBBLEMAKER

1) Make a wire square.
2) Cut an 8 inch piece of string, and tie its ends to make a loop.
3) Hang this loop from the center of the wire square as shown. Do not tie it tight, but let it hang loosely.
4) Dip this in the bubble soup.
5) Pick it up and poke a hole in the soap film in the center of the loop.
6) Watch what happens to the shape of the loop.

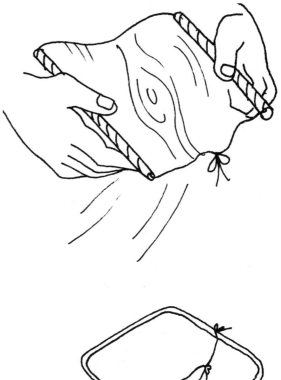

1.

What's Happening?
When soap is added to water, it lowers the surface tension of water. This means the molecules of the water hold together less tightly, making the water stretchy. This allows you to blow bubbles. Glycerine keeps the mixture from evaporating and helps the bubbles last longer. In the square wire frame, the surface tension of the soap film pulls on the string. Since the surface tension pulls equally in all directions, the string formed a circle shape.

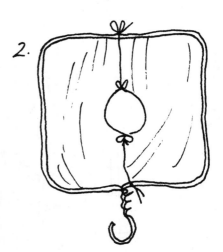

2.

Investigation

Rain-catching

Measure the amount of rain that falls with this simple rain measure called a rain gauge.

You need:
- widemouth jar
- narrow jar (olive jar is good)
- water
- funnel
- ruler
- masking tape
- fine-point permanent marker

Any luck, Froggy?

1) Mark 1 inch from the bottom of the widemouth jar. Fill it to that point with water.

2) Put a piece of tape up the side of the narrow jar. Pour in the water from the large jar.

3) On the tape, mark the level of this water.

4) Divide the space between that mark and the bottom of the jar into ten equal parts and mark each one. Mark ten more spaces of the same size above the line. This jar will be your measuring jar.

5) The widemouth jar will be your collecting jar. Place it outside on a rainy day.

6) At the end of the day, pour the rain into the measuring jar to see how much it has rained. Each mark on your measuring jar stands for 1/10 of an inch of rain on your gauge.

Investigation

Snow-catching

This simple snowcatcher will help you find out just how big that snowstorm was today!

You need:
- large coffee can
- ruler
- permanent marker

1) Use the marker to mark inches on the outside of the can.

2) Set the can outdoors on a snowy day. Place it away from buildings and trees in a spot that is not windy.

3) When the snow stops or the day ends, look to see how much snow has collected.

4) Let it melt at room temperature, and you'll find out how the snowfall compares to rain. Ten inches of snow is equal to about 1 inch of rain.

Investigation

181

Balloon Barometer

This simple barometer tells you whether the air pressure is rising or falling. That gives you some hints about upcoming weather!

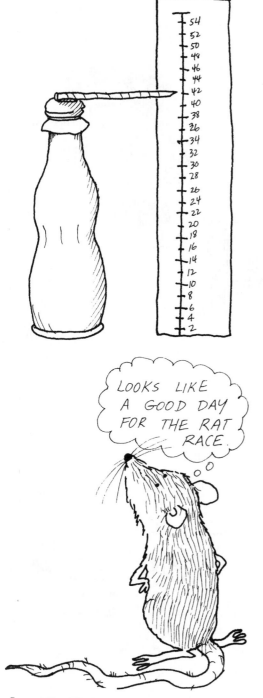

LOOKS LIKE A GOOD DAY FOR THE RAT RACE.

You need:

- drinking straw
- scissors
- white glue
- rubber band
- marker
- balloon
- poster board
- glass bottle
- ruler
- tape

1) Cut a piece of rubber from the balloon and fasten it tightly to the bottle with a rubber band.

2) Cut one end of the straw to a point. Glue the other end to the center of the stretched balloon.

3) Make a scale on a strip of poster board as shown.

4) Set the barometer near to the scale so the straw almost touches it. This needs to be in a place where the temperature stays about the same most of the time.

5) Wait for a clear day. Check the newspaper to see what the air pressure is, and mark that number where the straw is pointing.

6) Watch each day to see where the straw has moved. Do you see any connections between weather changes and barometer changes?

What's Happening?

As air pressure increases, it pushes down on the rubber and causes the straw's other end to move up. With a decrease in pressure, the balloon rises and the straw falls. An increase signals fair weather coming, a decrease signals bad weather.

Investigation

Speeding Air

Here's how you can make an anemometer to check out the speed (velocity) of wind or other moving air.

You need:
- adult help
- 2 table tennis balls
- sharp knife with ragged edge
- watch with second hand
- 2 wooden dowels (1" diameter) 12" long
- block of wood
- 1 wooden dowel (2" diameter) 24" long
- short nails
- long nails
- hammer
- candle
- red paint
- brush

ATTACH DOWEL TO SIDE OF BALL.

IT WORKS LIKE A CHAMP!

1) Nail the long dowel to the wooden block. Use a large nail to poke a hole into one end of this dowel.

2) Use the knife to cut both balls in half. Paint one half red. When it's dry, nail all the halves to the ends of the thin dowels.

3) Pound a long nail exactly through the center of both dowels as shown.

4) Wax the end of this nail with candle wax and set it in the hole at the end of the long dowel.

5) Hold this out the window of a car while someone is driving 10 mph. Count the revolutions of the red ball for 1 minute. Divide the number by ten. This will tell you how many revolutions it makes per mph of wind speed.

6) Now you're ready to check wind speed. Set the anemometer outside and count the revolutions in a minute. Can you figure out how fast the wind is blowing?

Investigation

183

Which Wind?

Did you know that wind comes in several sizes? Here's how you can keep track of which size it's wearing today.

You need:
- crayons or fine-point markers
- pen
- "Of Gentle Breezes & Hurricanes" data sheet

1) Choose a month for keeping track of the wind. Make a large calendar for that month. Make large squares for each day.

2) Watch the wind every day. Go out and feel it, watch the trees, and watch a wind vane or anemometer.

3) Use the wind scale on the data sheet to estimate the wind speed. Name the wind and record it on your calendar.

Investigation

Of Gentle Breezes & Hurricanes

Beaufort Wind Scale

0	CALM	under 1 mph	smoke rises straight up
1	LIGHT AIR	1-3 mph	smoke drifts
2	SLIGHT BREEZE	4-7 mph	leaves rustle
3	GENTLE BREEZE	8-12 mph	leaves move constantly flags fly
4	MODERATE BREEZE	13-18 mph	dust, loose leaves, paper raised up
5	FRESH BREEZE	19-24 mph	small trees sway
6	STRONG BREEZE	25-31 mph	large branches move hard to use an umbrella
7	MODERATE GALE	32-38 mph	whole trees sway hard to walk
8	FRESH GALE	39-46 mph	twigs break off trees
9	STRONG GALE	47-54 mph	slight damage to buildings
10	WHOLE GALE	55-63 mph	trees uprooted
11	STORM	64-72 mph	widespread damage
12	HURRICANE	over 72	severe, devastating damage

Make a calendar for the month.

Each day, record:

- estimated speed of wind
- number and name of wind
- picture of what wind is doing

185

Data Sheet

Cloudy With A Chance Of Weather

Be a weather watcher for a month, and you might turn out to be pretty good at predicting the weather, too.

You need:
- current calendar
- small notebook
- pens
- markers
- "Weather Watch" data sheet

1) Choose a month you'll be able to watch the weather every day. Fill in the dates on the calendar found on the data sheet.

2) Make a weather watcher's notebook using copies of the sample page from the data sheet.

3) Each day, draw a picture on the weather calendar chart (see data sheet).

4) Also, make notes in the weather watcher's notebook. It's a good idea to record the weather at the end of the day so you've had time to see what's happened.

5) At the end of the month, count to see how many days of rain, snow, sunshine, clouds, etc., you've had. Or, make other generalizations about the month's weather.

Investigation

Weather Watch

Each day, draw a picture of the weather and record weather data in your notebook.

Weather Watcher's Notebook

Today's Date: _____
Time of Record: _____
Temperature: (high/low) _____
Clouds: _____
Wind: (speed + direction) _____
Precipitation: (kind + amount) _____
Humidity: _____
Other: _____
_____

How many days of: →

Month of: _____

Sunday	Monday	Tuesday	Wednesday	Thursday	Friday	Saturday

Data Sheet

Just Plane Stuff

Try out a few of these flying objects, and learn some fascinating facts about what makes things fly.

You need:
- typing paper
- scissors
- drinking straws
- thread
- construction paper
- ruler
- tape
- paper clips
- tissue paper
- glue

Paper Race
1) Wad one piece of typing paper.

2) Stand up on a table, and drop the wadded paper and one flat sheet of paper at the same time. Which one reaches the floor first? What happens to the other one?

Parachute
1) Cut four 8 inch pieces of thread and one 12 inch square of tissue paper.

2) Tape one piece of thread to each corner of the square. Tie the ends of the thread together.

3) Make a small sky diver from construction paper, and glue a paper clip on the back.

4) Drop the parachute from a high place and watch.

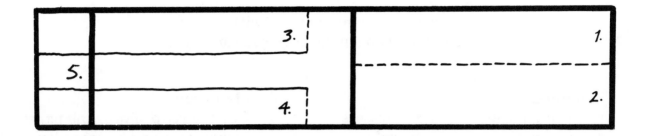

Helicopter

1) Copy the helicopter pattern from this page.

2) Cut on the outside heavy line.

3) Cut on the dotted lines.

4) Fold on the solid lines. Fold flap 1 toward you and flap 2 away from you.

5) Fold flaps 3 and 4 toward you. Then fold flap 5 up toward you.

6) Stand on a table, lift the helicopter high above you, and drop it.

What's Happening?

Air resists objects moving through it. There is more resistance as an object's surface area gets larger. The crumpled paper has less surface moving through the air than the flat sheet, so it falls to the ground faster. Gravity pulls down on the parachute, but air is caught under it. This air pushes up and slows the fall. Air also pushes on the rotors of the helicopter and keeps it afloat. Since each rotor on the helicopter is bent a different way, the air pushes opposite ways on each one and causes the helicopter to spin.

Investigation

189

Easy Gliders

Gliders are planes that fly without motors.
Here are two simple ones you can make.

You need:
- typing paper
- markers
- plastic straws
- drawing paper
- scissors
- ruler
- tape
- pencil

Circle Flyer

1) Cut one strip of drawing paper 1 1/2 inches wide and 7 inches long. Cut another strip the same width 9 inches long.

2) Tape both strips into loops. Then tape them to the ends of a straw.

3) Fly the glider by tossing it forward with the small loop in the front.

SQUAWK

Super Looper

1) Follow these directions to make a super looper glider. When you're finished, decorate, and test-fly it.

   A. Lay a piece of typing paper on the table longways, and fold it down the center. Open it.

   B. Along the longest edge, fold an even fold of about a half inch. Fold it again three or four times.

   C. Test-fly the paper to see if it will glide through the air. If it has been folded too many times, it will be too heavy and dive to the ground. If it wobbles or doesn't glide smoothly, it hasn't been folded enough.

   D. Fold the paper in half again, and cut as shown.

   E. Open the glider, and fold the edges of the tail and wings.

What's Happening?

To fly through the air, airplanes need to have something called lift. Lift results when the air pressure is greater beneath the wings than above. The shape of airplanes and their wings is designed to cause air to move faster above than below. This makes the pressure underneath the wings greater and causes the lift. Planes without motors can't fly too long because they eventually slow down to a speed that eliminates the lift.

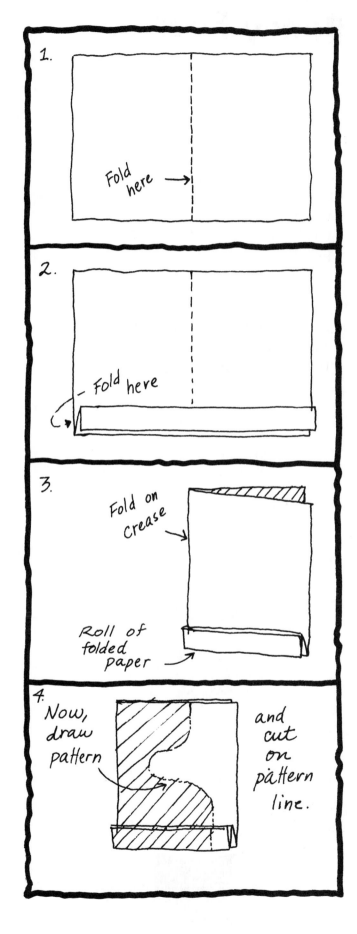

Investigation

Fancy Flier

This glider is a more sophisticated one that lets you control the direction it flies.

You need:
- typing paper
- markers
- pencil
- scissors
- ruler

1) Cut a shape from the pattern on page 193. Fold three to four half inch folds along the long front edge. (See page 191 for more directions.)

2) Cut two slits in the tail along the solid lines. If you bend each section on the dotted lines, this creates elevators on the tail.

3) Test-fly the glider with one elevator bent up, both elevators bent up, and both down.

4) Cut two slits in the back of the wings along the solid lines. If you bend each section on the dotted lines, this creates ailerons on the wings.

5) Test-fly the glider with the right aileron bent up, left down, left aileron up, and right down.

What's Happening?
When the elevators are up, air catches against them and pushes the tail down. This makes the front of the glider climb. When the elevators are down, air pushes up on the tail from underneath, and the glider goes down. Ailerons help the glider turn. Air gets trapped in front of an aileron that's up and pushes that wing down. On the side where the aileron is down, air gets trapped under the wing and pushes up. This tips the glider and causes it to turn. The plane turns right when the right aileron is up and the left one is down. Reverse the ailerons, and it turns left.

To make elevators, cut two slits on the solid lines shown on the tail. Then fold on the dotted lines.

To make ailerons, cut two slits on the solid lines shown on the wings. Then fold on the dotted lines.

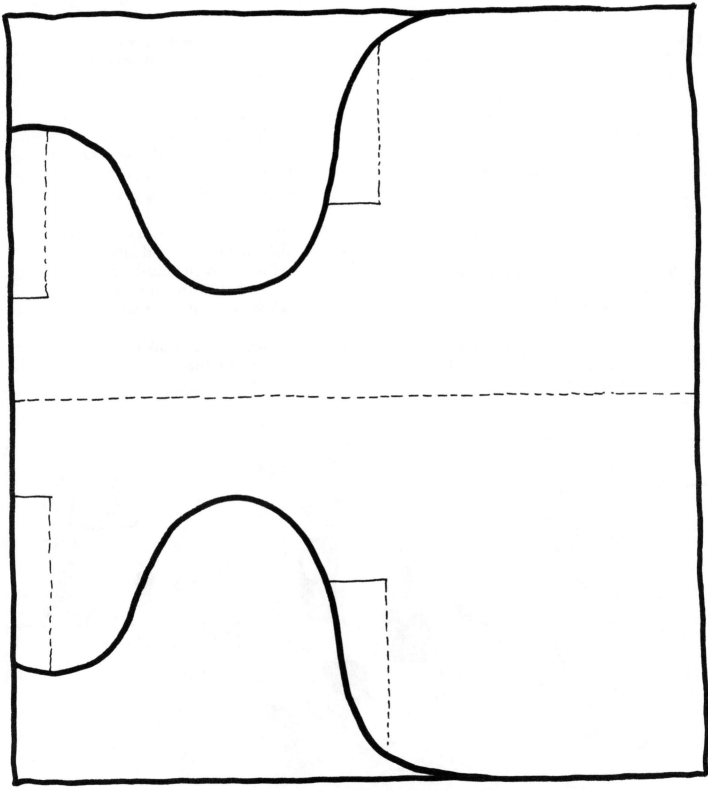

Data Sheet

Don't Take Rocks For Granite

Rocks may look ordinary, but they're not. Start collecting some, and when you begin to look at each one closely, you'll notice how special each one really is.

You need:
- cloth sack or pillowcase
- old rag
- shovel
- hammer
- "Private Rock Collection" data sheet
- pens
- markers
- labels
- book about rocks and minerals
- egg cartons

1) Go on a rock hunt. Take a cloth bag, hammer, shovel, and rag. Also take a set of cards copied from the data sheet.

2) Look around your neighborhood in fields, gardens, or empty lots. If possible, search in parks, on beaches, or forests. Pick up some samples of different kinds of rocks.

3) To get small samples, wrap a larger rock in a cloth, and break it with a hammer.

4) Label each sample with a number, and record it on a rock collector's card (see data sheet). Clean it off, and keep it in a section of an egg carton.

5) Examine each sample carefully. Look at the color and luster (shine). Test the hardness (see page 197), feel its weight. Makes notes about it on its card.

6) Use a reference book about rocks and minerals to help you identify your samples.

Investigation

A Private Rock Collection

Make several copies of this card.
Fill one out for each of your rock samples.
Get a book about rocks and minerals from the library.
It will help you identify your samples.

Number _____

Where I found it _____

Color _____

Luster (Shiny or not shiny?) _____

Weight (Heavy or light?) _____

Hardness (See Scale on page 197.) _____

Minerals it might contain _____

_____

Data Sheet

Welcome To The Hard Rock Club

One way to identify rocks and minerals is to test the hardness of each one. Practice finding the hardness of some samples from your own collection.

NICE ROCK!

You need:
- samples of rocks and minerals
- penny
- pen knife
- flat piece of clear glass
- small stick-on labels
- pen
- "Scratchy Business" data sheet

1) Take some rocks or minerals from your rock collection. Label each sample with a number.

2) Try scratching to see if a mark can be made on the rock. A scratch is a groove or dig which can't be rubbed off. Scratch each sample with your fingernail, a penny, and a knife blade.

3) Also, check to see if each sample will scratch glass or will scratch the other samples.

4) Record all your tests on the data sheet. Use the hardness chart to help you make some hypotheses about what minerals each of your samples might contain.

Investigation

Scratchy Business

Do the scratch tests on each rock to find out about the hardness of each one.

ROCK NUMBER	CAN IT BE SCRATCHED BY:			WILL IT SCRATCH GLASS?
	fingernail?	penny?	knife?	
#1.				
#2.				
#3.				
#4.				
#5.				
#6.				
#7.				
#8.				
#9.				

Each mineral on the scale can scratch the minerals above it.

Hardness Scale

1	TALC	can be scratched with fingernail
2	GYPSUM	can be scratched with fingernail scratches talc
3	CALCITE	can be scratched with a penny
4	FLUORITE	can be scratched with a knife
5	APATITE	can be scratched with a knife
6	FELDSPAR	scratches glass
7	QUARTZ	scratches glass
8	TOPAZ	scratches quartz
9	CORUNDUM	scratches topaz
10	DIAMOND	scratches all others

Data Sheet

A Case Of Erosion

Erosion is the moving, changing, or wearing away of a part of the earth's surface. You can watch soil erosion happening...right in your own room.

You need:
- a large aquarium
- good soil
- sand
- clippings from a plant or bush
- watering can
- water
- "Earth On The Move" data sheet

1) Mix the sand and soil in equal parts. Put this mix in the aquarium, piling it high on one end to form a steep hill with a flat top.

2) Use the watering can to make it "rain" lightly on the soil. Watch what happens.

3) Next, observe what happens when you make it rain hard.

4) Plant some little clippings on the hilltop, and repeat the sprinkling. Try planting some on the hillside, also.

5) Watch where the soil goes, and describe what happens during the rain. Record your observations on the data sheet.

6) Experiment to find some ways to slow down the soil erosion.

What's Happening?
The running water carries away some of the soil as it travels down the slope. Making little ditches or dents for the plants or planting in mounds are some means of slowing erosion.

Investigation

Earth On The Move

Draw your hill scene as it looks in the aquarium.

What happens to the soil when it rains lightly? _____
_____

What happens with heavy rain? _____
_____

How do plants change the erosion process? _____
_____

Draw the results of erosion.

Experiment to find some ways to slow
erosion. Write your ideas.

_____

_____

_____

I SHOULD MAYBE GET OUT OF HERE!

Data Sheet

Stalactite or Stalagmite?

Those icicle-like things that hang around in caves are called stalactites and stalagmites. Make some of your own and learn which are which.

You need:
- Epsom salts
- heavy string
- scissors
- box
- food coloring
- warm water
- 6 quart jars
- metal nuts
- spoon

1) Make a model of a cave by cutting a cave-like opening in the end of a box. Leave the top off the box.

2) In each jar mix a heavy solution of Epsom salts and water. Keep adding salt until it won't dissolve anymore. Stir in some food coloring.

3) Cut three strings long enough to lay across the top of the box, and reach down to the bottom of the jars on either side. (You may try two or three strings in each jar.)

4) Tie a metal nut on both ends of each string.

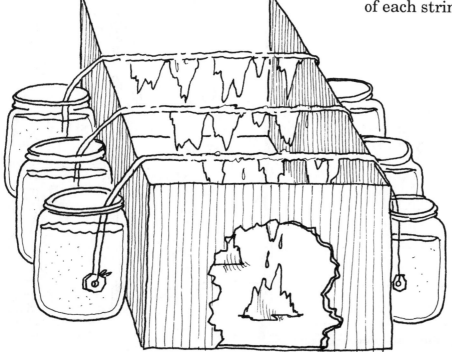

5) Lay the strings across the box so that the ends hang into the jars of salty water.

6) Leave the cave undisturbed for several weeks and watch what happens.

7) Every few days, draw a picture of what you see happening. This way you can keep a record of the growth of your stalactites and stalagmites.

What's Happening?
Both formations are made by the water dripping from the ceilings of the cave. This water is full of calcium. (Your experiment substitutes salt for the calcium.) As the calcium-heavy water evaporates, the calcium is left behind. Stalagmites are built up from the ground as the dripping water evaporates, and the stalactites grow down from the ceiling.

STALAGMITES - The G in the middle reminds you that these GROW up from the GROUND.

STALACTITES - The ending letters spell TITE, and the word has a C in it. This reminds you that they hang on TIGHTLY to the CEILING.

Investigation

Litter Brigade

One way people pollute the environment is by dropping stuff on the ground that doesn't belong there. It's called littering. Learn about litter, and clean up at the same time.

You need:
- a trash bag or a basket
- a partner
- gloves
- "Take Me To Your Litter" data sheet

1) Put on your gloves and go for a walk in a place that has litter. Fill your bag or basket with litter. But, don't pick up any broken glass or rusty cans.

2) Find a place where you can spread out your collection and look at it. What kinds of litter do you have? Paper? Wood? Cans? Bottles? Cloth?

3) Count the number of each kind. Use your data sheet to keep a record of your litter. Then complete the graph. Color each section to the correct height to show how much of each kind of litter you found.

4) Compare graphs with your classmates. What kinds of litter were most common? What does the litter tell you about the people who left it? What kinds of things were people doing there? What could be done to keep them from littering?

5) Collect litter in another place (a park, playground, city street, shopping mall, circus, theater). How is litter different?

Investigation

Take Me To Your Litter

Draw some of the litter here:

LITTER COUNT	
Kinds	**Number**
Cans	
Bottles or Glass	
Paper	
Cloth	
Wood	

MY LITTER GRAPH

	Cans	Glass	Paper	Cloth	Wood
35					
30					
25					
20					
15					
10					
5					
0					

Put Yourself In The Solar System

There's no better way to learn about our solar system than to put yourself right in the middle of it. Here's how!

You need:

- 11 people
- 1 lamp or lantern
- large space indoors
- labels or "costumes" for planets
- stopwatch
- lots of string or tape
- scissors
- reference book with diagram of the solar system

1) Choose one person to be the sun, one to be the moon, and one for each planet.

2) Use tape to mark a spot in the center of the room for the sun.

3) Lay out string or tape to mark an orbit for each planet to move around the sun. Use a reference book to see a diagram of planets and their orbits.

4) Make labels or costumes for the nine planets, the earth's moon, and the sun.

5) The person who is the sun should stand in the center of the room with a bright source of light.

6) Position the other planets in their orbits. The moon should stand near the earth.

7) Turn out the lights except for the sun's source. All planets should walk at a similar speed in their orbits around the sun.

8) The earth should turn (rotate) as he is moving in the orbit. The moon should travel around the earth as the earth moves on its orbit.

9) Talk about these things:

Moving at similar speeds, which planet gets around the sun first? Keep track of how long it takes each planet to get around the sun.

How much light does each planet get from the sun? Which part of the planet is dark?

Which planets get the strongest light?

10) Use the "Solar System Facts Chart" on page 239 to find information which will help you set up this investigation as well as learn some other interesting things about the solar system.

Investigation

A Simple Sun-clock

Long before fancy clocks and watches were invented, people used sundials to tell time. Here's one you can make and try out in your own backyard.

You need:

- pencil
- 10 inch square of wood
- protractor
- waterproof paint (2 colors)
- thin wooden dowel
- ruler
- compass
- hammer
- small brush
- wood glue

Making the Sun-clock

1) Paint the wood square and the dowel with waterproof paint. Let this dry well.

2) Use the compass to draw an 8 inch diameter circle on the wood. Draw a line to divide the circle in half.

3) Use the protractor to make a mark every 15° around half the circle. This will divide the half circle into 12 equal parts, one for each hour. You may mark half hours, also, if you wish.

4) Draw a straight line from the center of the circle to each of these marks, and paint all the lines with a fine paintbrush.

5) Paint the numbers as shown beginning with 6 a.m. on the left and ending with 6 p.m. on the right.

6) Use wood glue to attach the wooden dowel to the center of the circle. This is the gnomon of the sundial.

Telling Time With the Sun-Clock

1) Set the sun-clock outside in a spot that stays sunny all day.

2) Go outside at exactly noon. (Beware of daylight saving time when 1 p.m. is noon by the sun.)

3) Line up the sun-clock so the shadow of the gnomon falls right on the 12. Leave it in place, and you'll be able to tell the time as long as the sun is shining.

4) Compare the sun-clock with your watch at noon every few days, and adjust the sun-clock to keep it accurate.

What's Happening?

The rotation of the earth makes the sun appear to move in the sky each day. The earth takes 24 hours to make one complete rotation, so you are able to measure the time with a sundial divided into twenty-four parts (or twelve parts for the daylight hours).

Investigation

Quarters, Crescents, & Gibbouses

Spy on the moon. Not only will you learn about its phases, you'll also have a great excuse for staying up late.

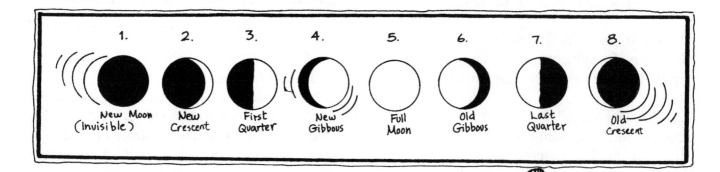

1. New Moon (Invisible)   2. New Crescent   3. First Quarter   4. New Gibbous   5. Full Moon   6. Old Gibbous   7. Last Quarter   8. Old Crescent

You need:
- black and white paint
- heavy cardboard circles (6 inches in diameter or larger) (Try to get circles from a pizza shop!)
- paintbrushes
- water
- string
- thumbtacks
- "Moonwatch" data sheet

1) Look carefully at the moon phases described on this page.

2) Make a sample of each one by painting a circle with black and white paint. (Let the paint dry between colors.) Label each phase.

3) Hang these from strings around your room so you'll learn what the phases look like.

4) Each night, look for the moon and draw a picture of what it looks like. Watch for at least 30 days. Use your moonwatch calendar to keep records.

What's Happening?
The moon is a sphere, so if it were in full view each night, it would look like a circle. But as the earth moves into different positions to cut off some of the sun's light from the moon, the moon appears to change shape.

Investigation

208

Moonwatch

Watch the moon for at least 30 days. Draw what you see each day and label your drawing with one of these:

N = new moon   **NC** = new crescent
FQ = first quarter   **NG** = new gibbous
F = full moon   **OG** = old gibbous
LQ = last quarter   **OC** = old crescent

Also, write the time the moon rises each night. (Or write "T" for nights when the moon came up too late for you to watch.)

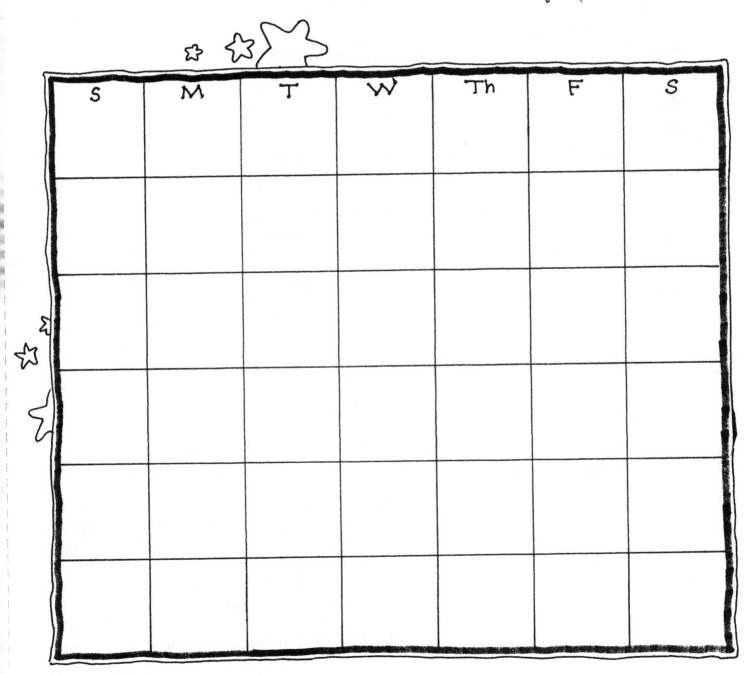

S	M	T	W	Th	F	S

How many days did each phase last?

Data Sheet

Indoor Constellations

You can't always be out under the night sky at the right time to see these constellations, so here's a way you can learn about them indoors, even in the daytime.

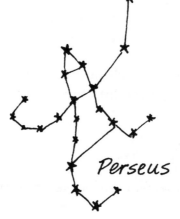

Perseus

Cassiopeia

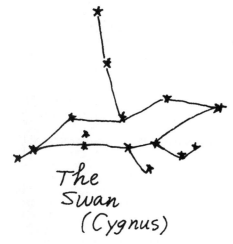

The Swan (Cygnus)

The Little Dipper

The Dragon (Draco)

You need:

- flashlight
- black paper
- compass
- straight pins
- small and large nails
- cardboard tube (4 to 6 inches in diameter)
- "The Scorpion & Other Night Sky Wonders" data sheets (pages 212-214)

- rubber bands
- paintbrush
- scissors
- black paint
- water
- tape
- large black plastic trash bag

1) Paint the inside of the cardboard tube black.

2) Cut several circles of black paper 2 inches larger in diameter than the tube.

3) Use straight pins and nails of different sizes to punch one constellation in each of the circles. Follow the constellation maps on the pages that follow this one. Make sure you label the circle with the constellation's name.

4) Tape the garbage bag to the wall.

Investigation

5) To view a constellation, fasten the circle over one end of the tube with a rubber band.

6) Turn out the lights and shine the flashlight into the open end of the tube. Point the tube toward the trash bag "screen."

7) Turn the tube around so you can see how the constellation looks from different viewpoints.

8) Repeat this process with several other constellations shown on the following pages.

What's Happening?
The light shines through the holes you punched and projects an enlarged map of the constellation onto the screen so you can see a replica of the constellation. Constellations do change locations in the sky with the seasons as the earth revolves around the sun in its orbit.

It's the Big Dipper, part of Ursa Major.

The Big Dipper

Investigation

The Scorpion & Other Night Sky Wonders

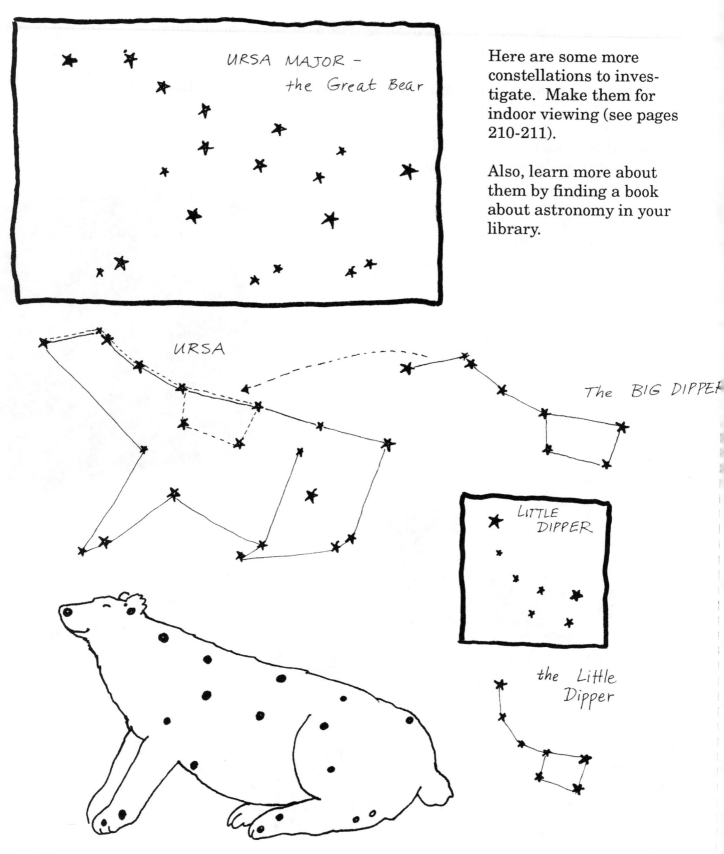

URSA MAJOR –
the Great Bear

Here are some more constellations to investigate. Make them for indoor viewing (see pages 210-211).

Also, learn more about them by finding a book about astronomy in your library.

URSA

The BIG DIPPER

LITTLE DIPPER

the Little Dipper

SCORPIUS

The Great Square

PEGASUS
(the winged horse)

GEMINI
(the twins)

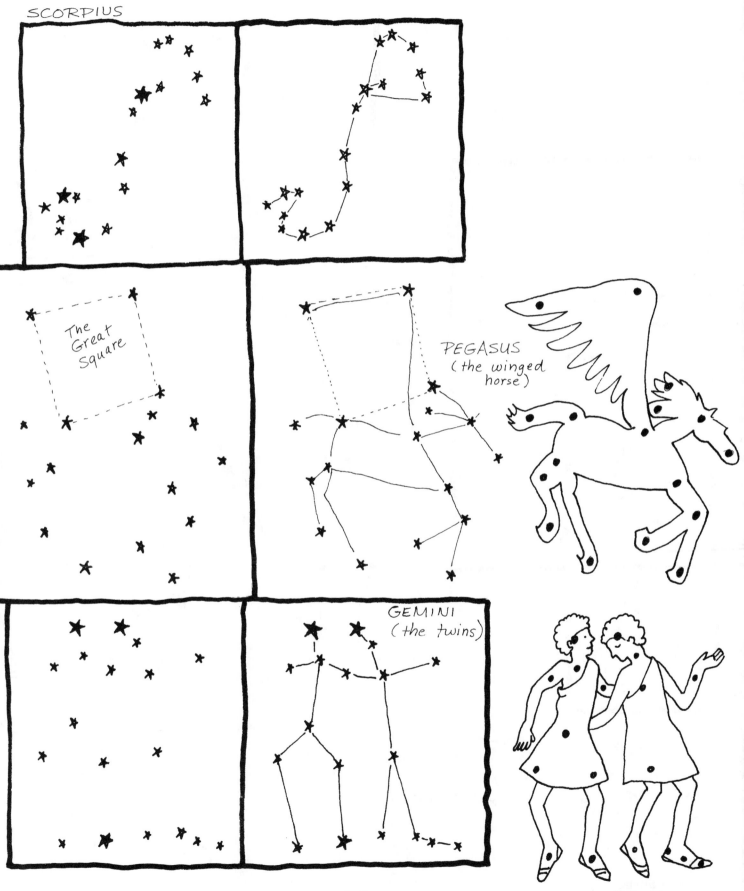

213

Data Sheet

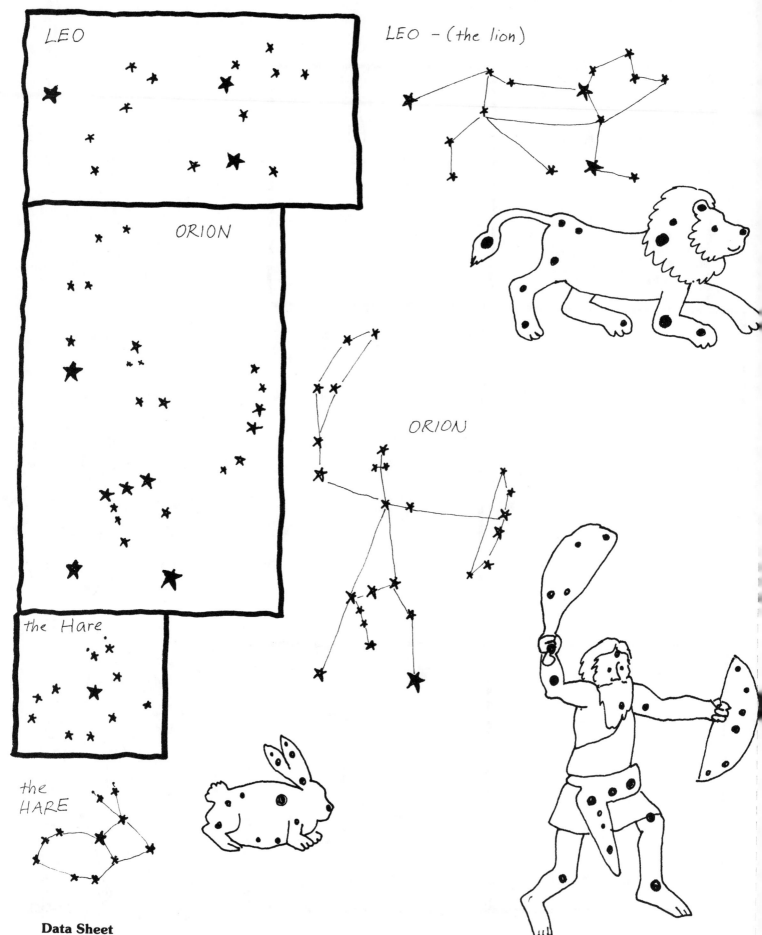

LEO

LEO – (the lion)

ORION

ORION

the Hare

the HARE

Science Words & Symbols & Such

Science Words To Know

abdomen—the third section of an insect's body; in humans, the part of the body between the chest and hips

absorb—to soak up

accelerate—to increase speed of movement or to increase speed of a chemical reaction

acid—a substance which tastes sour and turns litmus paper red

acid rain—a kind of environmental pollution caused when sulphur compounds, which are expelled into the air as waste products from industry, combine with rain water to form weak acids

adapt—to change in a way that fits changing environments or conditions

adaptation—a process by which living things change in an attempt to survive

adult—a fully mature plant or animal

aerobic—a plant or animal which needs oxygen to grow; a type of exercise which increases the body's demand for oxygen

aerodynamics—the study of the forces that act on objects moving through air

aileron—a movable flap on the wing of an airplane which allows the plane to turn

air—the mixture of gases that makes up the earth's atmosphere

air pressure—the pressure that air puts on everything

ailementary canal—the food tube which extends from the mouth to the anus

alkali—a base or substance that neutralizes an acid and turns litmus paper blue

alternating current—an electric current that flows first in one direction, then in the other

alternator—a generator that produces alternating electric current

altimeter—an instrument that measures height above sea level

altitude—the height of something above sea level

alveoli—tiny air sacs in the lungs through which oxygen is passed into blood vessels

amoeba—a one-celled microscopic organism

amphibian—a cold-blooded vertebrate which spends part of its life cycle living in water and part living on land

amplify—to make something (such as a sound) louder

antennae—a pair of feelers on the head of insects and a few other animals

antibiotic—a medicine derived from molds that kills bacteria in the body

antibody—a substance produced by the body that kills germs and helps protect against diseases

anther—the pollen-containing top of the stamen on a flower

anus—the opening at the end of the food canal through which undigested waste is expelled from the body of animals

aorta—the largest artery in the body. It is connected to the heart.

appendix—a tiny, finger-like tube found at the beginning of the large intestine

artery—one of many blood vessels that carries blood away from the heart to other parts of the body

arthropod—an animal with a jointed, hard outer skeleton or covering on the body

astronaut—a person who is trained to fly and explore in space

astronomy—the study of heavenly bodies

atmosphere—the mixture of gases that surrounds the earth or other planets

atom—the smallest particle of an element that has all the properties of that element

atomic energy—energy that is stored in the nucleus of an atom and can be released by fusion or fission reactions

atrium—one of the chambers of the heart

attraction—the force that draws two things together

autumnal equinox—a time in the fall when day and night are of the same length due to the sun's shining directly on the equator

axis—an imaginary line through the earth (or other body) on which the earth spins

bacteria—tiny organisms, some of which cause diseases

barometer—an instrument that measures air pressure

base—a chemical substance that neutralizes an acid and turns litmus paper blue. Bases react with acids to form a salt.

battery—two or more electric cells that make and store electricity

beam—a ray of light

biodegradable—something that can be broken down or decomposed by bacteria

biology—the study of living things

bird—a class of mammals that has wings, is covered with feathers, and lays eggs

blood—a fluid that flows through the vessels of many animals and carries needed substances to all parts of the body

bone—hard tissue which makes up the skeletons of vertebrates

botany—the study of plants

brain—a mass of nerve cells which controls all the life processes and is contained in the skull of many animals

bronchi—two main tubes branching off the windpipe (trachea) into the lungs

burn—to be set on fire or to be injured by heat

calorie—a unit used in measuring heat

camouflage—the colors or appearance of an animal's body which blend into the surroundings and thereby helps to protect the animal from its predators

capacity—the amount of space in something

capillary—a tiny blood vessel found in many animals

carbon—a chemical element found widely in plants, animals, and the environment

carbohydrates—a group of foods made by green plants which is necessary for animal nutrition

carbon dioxide—an odorless gas in the air which is made of carbon and oxygen

carnivore—an animal that eats meat

carpals—tiny bones in the wrist

cartilage—tough, elastic material that is attached to the joints of bones. It helps joints move smoothly.

cell—a small part of every living thing. Cells have an outer wall called a membrane and a "control center" called a nucleus. Cells are filled with living matter called protoplasm.

center of gravity—the point of an object at which the weight of the object balances perfectly

centigrade—a scale for measuring temperature on which water freezes at 0° and boils at 100°

central nervous system—made up of the brain and spinal cord in vertebrates. This controls the activities of the animal

centrifugal force—the force that appears to make something when rotated move out and away from the center

centripetal force—the force which pulls a body inward and keeps it moving in a curve around a central object

charge—an amount of electrical energy held within something; to fill something with electrical energy

chemistry—the study of substances and their reactions with other substances

chemical change—a combination or reaction of substances which results in a new substance

chlorophyll—the green substance in plants which uses the energy in sunlight to make food and oxygen

chromosomes—microscopic threadlike substances found in the nucleus of a cell which carry the characteristics of a living thing

circuit—a path along which electricity travels. Electricity will not flow unless the path is completely closed.

circulation—going around and around in the same place, such as the blood goes around the body in a system of vessels

circulatory system—all the organs and tissues in the body that make circulation of blood possible

classify—to group together objects that have similar characteristics

climate—the weather conditions that are usually found in an area

cloud—a collection of tiny drops of water that group together in the sky

cocoon—a case of threads which an animal spins around itself to make a home for the process of turning into an adult

cold-blooded—an animal whose body temperature changes as the temperature in the surrounding environment changes

colon—the large intestine

combustion—the process of a substance reacting with oxygen in the air to catch fire and burn

compass—an instrument that shows direction because it has a needle which always points to the magnetic North Pole

compound—a substance made up of two or more elements

condensation—the process of changing from a gas to a liquid

conductor—an object or material that carries electricity well

conduction—the movement of electricity or other energy through an object or material

conservation—the careful use and protection of plants, animals, and other aspects of the natural environment

constellation—a group of stars that forms a pattern or a shape in the sky

contract—to become smaller in size

convection—the movement of heat by currents through a gas or liquid

corpuscle—a red or white blood cell

crater—a deep bowl-shaped hollow in the earth or surface of another heavenly body

crescent—the curved, partial-circle shape that the moon is in its first and last quarters

crust—the outer layer of the earth

crustacean—an animal with a hard outer shell on its body

culture—a sample of microorganisms grown purposely for studying

current—the flow of electricity along a path; the movement of a gas or liquid in a particular direction

data—information and facts that have been gathered for purposes of studying something or drawing conclusions about something

decible—a unit for measuring the loudness of sounds

deciduous—plants that lose their leaves in the winter

decompose—to rot or decay

degree—a unit of measurement used to find temperature; a unit used for measuring angles and circles

density—the comparison of the mass of an object to its volume. The density of an object equals its mass divided by its volume.

diaphragm—the strong muscle layer that separates the chest from the abdomen and assists people in breathing

diffraction—the splitting of a ray of light into all the colors of the spectrum

diffusion—the spreading of a substance through a liquid or a gas

digestion—the process of breaking food down into substances small and simple enough for use by the body

digestive system—all the organs and tissues in the body which make digestion possible

dilute—to make a solution weaker by adding more solvent

dissect—to cut something into smaller parts in order to study it

dissolve—to cause a substance to break up and disappear in a liquid

DNA (deoxyribonucleic acid)—a substance found in the nucleus of cells which holds the plan for the inherited characteristics of any individual living thing

drought—a long period of weather with very little or no rain

earth—the planet on which we live

eclipse—a shadow cast by one body in space on another which blocks or partially blocks our view of the body

ecology—the study of the relationship between living things and between living things and their natural environment

ecosystem—a community of living things and the environment in which they live

electric charge—an amount of electricity stored in something

electricity—energy carried by the movement of free electrons

electrodes—two rods that carry electric current in and out of the electrolyte in a battery

electrolyte—the liquid or paste in a battery in which chemical changes take place to produce electricity

electromagnet—an iron rod with many coils of wire wrapped around it and an electric current passing through it

electron—a negatively charged particle which orbits the nucleus of an atom

embryo—the earilest stage of development of a plant or animal beginning with the fertilization of the egg cell

element—a simple substance made of atoms of one type

elevators—flaps on the tail of an airplane that assist the plane in climbing or descending

endocrine system—the glands in the body that produce hormones

energy—the potential to do work or cause change

environment—all the surroundings and conditions in which a plant or animal lives

enzymes—chemicals in the body that control different reactions in the body such as the breaking down and digestion of food

epidermis—the outer layer of skin or tissue in plants and animals

epiglottis—the flap which covers the opening to the larynx and prevents food from getting into the windpipe

equator—the imaginary line around the earth which is equidistant from the north and south poles

equilibrium—a state of balance between forces

erosion—the wearing away of the earth's surface by water or wind

esophagus—the tube that carries food from the mouth to the stomach

eustachian tube—a tube that leads from the ear to the throat

evaporation—the changing of a liquid into a gas

exhale—to breathe out

exoskeleton—a hard outer covering on the bodies of some animals

expand—to get larger or spread out

experiment—a test done for the purpose of discovering something or proving something

Farenheit—a scale for measuring temperature on which water freezes at 32° and boils at 212°

family—a category used for classifying a group of living things

fault—a crack in the earth's crust between masses of moving rock

femur—the long bone in the upper leg

fertilize—to join together male and female reproductive cells to begin the growth of a new living thing; to add nutrients to soil in order to make it richer

fever—a body temperature higher than the normal 98.6°F

fibula—one of the two long bones in the lower leg

filament—a very thin wire in an electric light bulb that glows when electric current passes through it

filter—to separate a solid that has not dissolved from a liquid or a solid from air by passing the mixture through some material that holds out the solid

fish—a cold-blooded vertebrate with fins and gills that lives in water

fission—a process where the nuclei of very heavy atoms (usually uranium or plutonium) are split to produce energy by bombarding them with neutrons

flammable—able to burn easily

flexible—able to bend without easily breaking

float—to stay on the surface of a liquid or slowly drift in the air

flower—the part of a seedbearing plant which makes reproduction possible

fog—a weather condition in which water vapor near the ground condenses into tiny drops of water and clings to particles of dust or dirt in the air

food chain—a chain or series of living things which eat each other for energy

force—any action or power that starts or stops the movement of a body or changes its direction or speed

formula—chemical letters and symbols written to show the composition of a compound; a set of symbols that shows how to solve a math problem

fossil—the hard remainder or impression of a living thing preserved in a rock

frequency—the number of times something happens in a given period

friction—a force that occurs when two things are rubbed together. It generally slows down one or more of the objects and produces heat.

fulcrum—the support point for a lever

fungus—a simple plant that usually lives off dying or dead plants or animals and reproduces by means of spores

fusion—the process of joining two atomic nuclei together which releases energy

galaxy—a system of planets, stars, and other bodies in space. Our galaxy is The Milky Way.

gale—a strong wind that blows at speeds between 32 to 63 mph

gas—a state of matter that has mass but no shape of its own filling whatever container it is in

gender—the sex of an animal, male or female

gene—a part of a chromosome that controls a particular characteristic in a living organism

generator—a machine that transforms kinetic energy into electrical energy

genetics—the study of genes and inherited characteristics

geology—the study of the earth

germ—a microscopic, one-celled organism that causes disease

germination—the beginning of growth

glacier—a river of ice that moves very slowly

glider—an aircraft or other object that moves smoothly through the air without the help of a motor

granite—a type of hard igneous rock

gravity—force of attraction between any two objects which have mass

habitat—the place where a plant or animal lives or grows naturally

hail—a kind of precipitation made up of small pieces of ice

health—the absence of disease in living organisms

heart—the muscular organ that pumps blood through the body

helium—a chemical element which is a gas lighter than air

hemisphere—half of the earth as divided by the equator or dateline

herbivore—an animal whose only food is plants

heredity—passing characteristics from one generation of living things to another

hibernation—an inactive state which some animals pass into in the winter

hormones—chemicals in the body which regulate certain processes such as growth and development

horsepower—a unit of measurement for determining the power of an engine

humus—a blackish-brown organic material that results when leaves and plants decay

hydroelectricity—electrical energy that is produced by the action of moving water

hygiene—the process of keeping your body clean and healthy

ice—frozen water

igneous—a kind of rock formed by the cooling of hot liquid (magma) that comes from a volcano

ignite—to set something on fire

immunity—the ability of plants and animals to fight off certain diseases or other foreign materials that enter the cells

incisors—four sharp, pointed teeth found near the front of the mouth in mammals

incubation—a process of keeping eggs warm until they are ready to hatch

inertia—the tendency for a moving object to keep moving or a resting object to remain at rest

infection—a disease caused by germs

inflammable—something that can be easily set on fire

inflate—to fill with air or another gas

inherit—to receive the characteristics of parents through reproductive cells

inorganic—substances which are not made by living things but are usually made up of minerals

insect—an animal belonging to a group which has three body parts (head, abdomen, thorax), six legs, a hard exoskeleton, and in most cases two pairs of wings

instinct—an automatic behavior that does not have to be learned

insulator—a material that does not allow energy (usually electricity or heat) to pass through it

intensity—the amount of light, heat, or loudness of sound

intestine—a part of the food tube that extends from the stomach to the anus

invertebrate—an animal that has no backbone

iodine—a chemical element used to indicate the presence of starches

ion—an atom or group of atoms with either a positive or negative electrical charge

joint—a mechanism in the body where two bones come together allowing the bones to move freely. Hinge joints swing back and forth. Ball and socket joints allow one bone to rotate in the other.

kidneys—two organs in the body that filter out waste products from the blood

laboratory—a place set up for carrying out scientific work and experiments

larva—a worm-like organism that is part of the life cycle of insects

lava—hot, melted rock that is forced out of a volcano; rocks formed from cooling, liquid lava

leaf—a part of a plant that contains chlorophyll and makes the food necessary for the plant's growth by a process called photosynthesis

lever—a simple machine that allows something to be lifted with less effort

life cycle—the stages and changes a living thing passes through as it develops from a fertilized egg into an adult

ligament—strong, flexible tissue that holds bones together at joints

lightning—a flash of light in the sky caused by a large spark of electricity traveling between two clouds or between a cloud and the ground

liquid—a state of matter which has mass and takes the shape of the container into which it is placed

litmus paper—paper treated with a substance which allows it to be used in testing for acids and bases

litter—a type of pollution involving the deposit of nonorganic, nondecomposable junk and garbage around the natural environment

luminous—something that gives off light

lunar—relating to the moon

lungs—the organs in the body whose function is to breathe air

luster—the shininess of a mineral

machine—a device that does work by using some kind of energy

magma—melted rock found below the earth's crust; sometimes erupts through cracks in the crust

magnet—a piece of iron that can attract or repel some metals

magnetic field—the space around a magnet in which the magnet's force can act

magnetism—a property of some metals which allows them to attract or repel a piece of iron

magnify—to make something appear larger than it is

malnutrition—a condition in which an animal does not have enough of the kinds of food to keep it growing and healthy

mammal—a member of a class of warm-blooded vertebrate animals covered with hair or fur, and in most cases the females give birth to live babies.

mantle—the layer of the planet earth that lies below its crust

marine—relating to the sea or something that lives in the sea

mass—the amount of matter in an object or body

matter—the material of which everything is made. All matter is either solid, liquid, or gas.

mechanical energy—energy of motion, also called kinetic energy

medicine—the study of diseases and prevention of diseases; a treatment used to prevent, heal, or aid pain or illness

melt—to change from a solid into a liquid

Mercury—the smallest planet in the solar system which is also the closest planet to the sun

metamorphic rock—a kind of rock changed by heat or pressure

metacarpals—the bones of the hand

metamorphosis—the change in form some animals go through as they grow from a fertilized egg to an adult

metatarsals—the bones of the foot

meteor—a piece of matter traveling in space that burns up upon entering the earth's atmosphere

meteorite—the unburned portion of a meteor that falls to the earth's surface

microorganism—a living thing so small it can only be seen under a microscope

migrate—to move from one place to another. Some animals migrate at certain times of the year to obtain better food supply.

mineral—a natural material found on the earth which does not come from plants or animals

mixture—a substance formed by the combination of two or more other substances that can be separated by physical means

molar—one of several large teeth with three roots found in the back of the mouth

mold—a fungus-type growth which can live and grow on organic material

molecule—the smallest part of an element or compound that has all the properties of that element or compound

molt—to shed feathers, skin, or other outer coverings of the body

momentum—the force of a moving body determined by multiplying the body's mass with its velocity

motor—a machine that changes electrical or chemical energy into mechanical energy

moon—a heavenly body which revolves around any of the planets

natural—something produced by nature as opposed to something that is man-made

nectar—a sweet liquid made by some flowers to attract insects so they will pollinate other flowers by carrying pollen which sticks to the insects as they go to the nectar in other flowers

nerve—a group of fibers which carries messages between the brain and other parts of the body

nervous system—a system including the brain, spinal cord, and other nerve cells which controls all the actions of the body

neutral—a chemical substance which is neither acid or alkaline

neutron—an uncharged particle found in the nucleus of all atoms except hydrogen

nitrogen—a chemical element that makes up three quarters of the earth's atmosphere. It is a gas with no odor, color, or taste.

nonconductor—a material or substance that does not carry a particular form of energy well such as electricity, heat, or sound; an insulator

nuclear energy—energy released when the nuclei of atoms split or join together

nucleus—the center of an atom which contains all the protons and neutrons present in the atom

nutrition—all the processes and functions involved with eating and digesting food

observation—watching or studying something very closely

opaque—a substance that light cannot pass through

optic—relating to the eyes

optic nerve—the nerve that carries messages between the retina of the eye and the brain

orbit—the path a planet or satellite follows as it moves around another body in space

organ—a part of the body with a specific function

organic—relating to plants or animals

organism—a living plant or animal

ovary—the female cells in plants or animals which produce cells or eggs that can be fertilized

oxidation—combining a substance with oxygen

ozone—a gas (O_3) found in the upper atmosphere of the earth which filters the sun's ultraviolet rays

pancreas—a gland in the abdomen that secretes insulin and several digestive juices

parasite—an organism that lives on or in another organism and depends on the other for food and shelter

particle—a very small piece of material or matter

patella—the kneecap

perimeter—the outside edge of a figure or the distance around the outside edge of a figure

petal—a brightly-colored part of a flower that by its color and the sweet nectar it holds attracts insects which help pollinate other flowers

phalanges—toe and finger bones

phase—a stage in the changes that occur in the visibility of the moon from earth

photosynthesis—the process by which green plants are able to use sunlight energy to make plant food from carbon dioxide and water

physics—the study of matter, energy, and forces

physiology—the study of the way living organisms work and function

pigment—a substance that gives color to some part of a plant or animal

pitch—the highness or lowness of a sound

planet—a body in space that revolves around the sun

pole—the northern or southern-most end of the earth; one of the ends of a magnet where the magnetic force is strongest

pollen—tiny grains produced by flowering plants which carry the male reproductive cells

pollination—the fertilizing of a plant ovum (female reproductive cell) by pollen

pollution—poisoning or harming a part of the natural environment

porous—something full of tiny holes or pores liquids or gases can pass through

precipitate—a substance which separates from a solution and settles to the bottom of the container

precipitation—some form of moisture falling from the air, i.e., rain, snow, sleet, hail, mist, fog, etc.

pressure—a pushing force or the measurement of a pushing force

prey—an animal that is hunted or eaten by another animal

prism—a geometric space figure which has two triangular bases and three rectangular sides. A glass prism bends a ray of light in such a way to separate it into the colors of the spectrum.

property—a characteristic of a substance

propulsion—a force which pushes an object such as an airplane, forward

protein—a group of complicated molecules made up of amino acids, a basic part of all living things

proton—a positively-charged particle in the nucleus of an atom

protozoa—a one-celled microscopic animal

pupa—a stage in the development of some insects in which the insect is inside a hardened covering for a period of time and from which an adult form of the insect emerges

pupil—the hole in the center of the eye through which light passes

radiation—energy given out from a source of heat or light - also harmful energy given off by radioactive materials, i.e., x rays, gamma rays, etc.

radioactive—an element or substance which gives off harmful radiation

radium—a radioactive metal found in the earth in ore

radius—the outer bone of the lower arm

rainbow—an arc formed in the sky when the sun shines on raindrops at an angle which breaks the sunlight into the colors of the spectrum

ratio—a comparison of two numbers or amounts

ray—a line which represents the movement of light or some motion

reaction—the effect which occurs when two substances are combined

record—to write down observations or information

rectum—the lower end of the large intestine

recycle—to use a substance over again

red blood cell—a plate-shaped red cell which carries oxygen to the body's cells

reflection—bouncing back of a light beam or a sound wave

reflex—an automatic reaction in the body which happens in response to certain stimuli

refraction—the bending of a light ray that occurs when it passes through certain substances

repel—to push or move away

reproduce—to create offspring like the parents

reproductive system—all the organs, glands, and tissues in a plant or animal which make it possible to create offspring

resistance—something that works against a force to slow it down

respiration—the breathing process

respiratory system—all the organs and tissues in an animal that make breathing possible

retina—the layer of the inner eye sensitive to light

revolve—to move in an orbit around another object

ribs—the curved bones which attach to the backbone and wrap around the front of the body to form the chest

root—the bottom part of a plant that usually grows into the soil and absorbs water and food from the soil

rot—to decompose or decay with the help of tiny organisms

saline—a salty solution

saliva—a liquid produced by glands in the mouth that helps to digest food

satellite—a body that orbits around another body in space

saturate—to fill a liquid or gas so full it cannot absorb any more

scapula—shoulder blade

secrete—a cell, gland, or an organ giving off a substance

sediment—solid particles which settle to the bottom of a liquid or are deposited by water or wind

sedimentary rock—rocks formed by particles of sand or rock dropped by wind or moving water

seed—a fertilized cell that will develop into a new plant or animal

sense—one of the five ways animals perceive their environment: sight, hearing, touch, smell, taste

sensory—anything that has to do with the senses or the receiving of stimuli

sepal—a part of a flower which lies at the bottom of the petals

shadow—a dark area caused when one object blocks some of the light falling on another object or area

sink—to settle below the surface of a liquid

skin—the soft outer covering of humans and some other animals

soil—small particles which make up the outermost layer of the earth's surface

solar—relating to the sun

solar system—the sun and all the planets that orbit around it

solid—a substance that has a definite shape and volume

soluble—a substance capable of dissolving in a liquid

solution—a liquid in which something has been dissolved

source—the place from which something starts

space—an empty area; the area outside the earth's atmosphere

species—a group in which animals or plants are classified

specimen—small sample, organism, or item used as a representative of others like it for study purposes

spectrum—the colors seen when light is separated as it passes through glass or water

speed—the distance a moving object travels divided by the time it took it to get there

sphere—a ball-shaped object

spinal column—the backbone of a vertebrate animal

spinal cord—a thick mass composed of many nerve tissues which runs through the spinal column and connects the brain to all parts of the body through a system of nerves

spore—a type of reproductive cell produced by many plants

stalactite—a solid lime deposit which hangs down from the roof of a cave

stalagmite—a solid lime deposit which builds up from the floor of a cave

stalk—the main, thickest part of a plant stem

stamen—a slender stalk of a flower which is the male part that produces pollen

star—a body in space made up of very hot gases; its appearance is very shiny

steam—water vapor, an invisible gas

stem—the main stalk of a plant

stigma—the part of the flower, usually at the top of the style, where pollen sticks when the flower is pollinated

stomach—an organ part of the digestive system in which food is held for several hours and is partially digested by strong juices

style—a slender, stalk-like part of a flower that usually holds the stigma

sun—a large star around which all the planets in our solar system revolve. The sun provides light and heat needed to sustain life on earth.

surface—the outside layer or area of an object or living thing

surface tension—a property of liquids in which there appears to be a thin film or elastic covering on the top of the liquid that holds the molecules of the liquid together slightly

suspension—a substance made up of particles of a solid spread equally throughout a liquid but not dissolved in it

symbiosis—a relationship in which two organisms live off one another, each benefitting the other

symbol—a sign or letter that stands for something

synthetic—a substance made artificially and not found naturally

tactile—something that can be felt by the sense of touch

tarsals—the heel and ankle bones

taste—the sense that determines sourness, sweetness, bitterness, or saltiness by means of taste buds on the tongue

taste bud—a group of cells on the tongue that senses taste

tear—salty liquid secreted by the eyes to keep them moist and clean

tear duct—small tube that runs from the corner of the eye to the back of the nose

telescope—an instrument which uses a series of mirrors and lenses to make distant objects appear closer and larger

temperature—the hotness or coldness of something, usually measured by a thermometer in degrees

tendon—a strong tissue that attaches a muscle to bones

theory—an idea that seems to explain why something happens

thermal—having to do with heat or temperature

thermal energy—energy that comes from some form of heat

thermometer—a device used for measuring temperature

thorax—the middle segment of an insect between the head and the abdomen

thrust—the force which moves something forward

thunder—a loud rumbling sound in the sky caused by air heating and expanding suddenly

tibia—the large bone (shinbone) of the lower leg

tissue—a group of cells that makes up a body organ such as muscle, skin, bone

tongue—the body's organ that senses taste

topsoil—the top layer of soil on the earth's surface

torque—a force which causes something to rotate or spin

toxic—a substance which is harmful or poisonous to humans or other animals

trachea—the windpipe which carries air from the mouth to the lungs

transfusion—transferring blood from one person to another

translucent—a material through which some light passes but which is not transparent

transparent—a material light passes through to allow someone to see through it

transpiration—the loss of moisture from the leaves of plants

ulna—the inner bone of the lower arm

universe—all the bodies in outer space

vacuum—a space with no air in it

vapor—the gas form of a material that is usually liquid

vein—a blood vessel that carries blood to the heart; a small food-carrying tube found in the leaves of plants

velocity—speed

ventricle—a chamber of the heart

vertebra—one of the many small bones that make up the backbone

vertebrate—an animal that has a backbone

vibrate—to move quickly back and forth

virus—a very small living organism that lives off the cells of an animal or plant

vision—the sense of sight

volcanic rock—rock formed by hardened lava from a volcano

volcano—an opening in the earth's crust through which molten rock (lava) is forced

volt—a unit of measuring the strength of a flow of electricity, electromotive force.

volume—the space taken up by matter

warm-blooded—an animal whose body temperature remains the same in any environment

waste—the products unused and expelled in some manner from the body; to make poor or careless use of resources

water vapor—the gaseous form of water

watt—a unit used for measuring electrical power

wave—a vibrating movement of something along a path

weather—the conditions in the atmosphere at a particular time

weight—the heaviness of an object or material

white blood cell—a blood cell which appears colorless and helps fight infection and diseases in the body

wind—moving air

windpipe— the tube that carries air from the mouth to the lungs; the trachea

x rays—high energy invisible light rays which can penetrate the soft tissues of the body

zygote—fertilized sex cell in a plant or animal

Units of Measurement

Measurement	Unit	Symbol
acceleration	meter per second^2	m/s^2
area	square millimeters	mm^2
	square centimeters	cm^2
	square meters	m^2
	hectares (10,000 m^2)	ha
	square kilometers	km^2
capacity	milliliter	ml
	liter	l
	kiloliter	kl
density	gram per cubic centimeter	c/cm^3
	kilogram per cubic meter	kg/m^3
electric current	ampere	A
electric potential	volt	V
electric power	watt	W
force	newton	N
length	millimeter	mm
	centimeter	cm
	meter	m
	kilometer	km
mass	milligram	mg
	gram	g
	kilogram	kg
	metric ton	t
pressure	pascal	Pa
velocity	meter per second	m/s^2
volume	cubic millimeters	mm^3
	cubic centimeters	cm^3
	cubic meters	m^3

Symbols for Elements

Ac	Actinium	Mg	Magnesium
Ag	Silver	Mn	Manganese
Al	Aluminum	Mo	Molybdenum
Ar	Argon	N	Nitrogen
As	Arsenic	Na	Sodium
At	Astatine	Nb	Niobium
Au	Gold	Ne	Neon
B	Boron	Ni	Nickel
Ba	Barium	O	Oxygen
Be	Beryllium	Os	Osmium
Bi	Bismuth	P	Phosphorus
Br	Bromine	Pb	Lead
C	Carbon	Pd	Palladium
Ca	Calcium	Po	Polonium
Cd	Cadmium	Pt	Platinum
Cl	Chlorine	Ra	Radium
Cr	Chromium	Rb	Rubidium
Cs	Cesium	Re	Rhenium
Cu	Copper	Rh	Rhodium
F	Fluorine	Rn	Radon
Fe	Iron	Ru	Ruthenium
Fr	Francium	S	Sulfur
Ga	Gallium	Sb	Antimony
Ge	Germanium	Sc	Scandium
H	Hydrogen	Se	Selenium
He	Helium	Si	Silicon
Hf	Hafnium	Sn	Tin
Hg	Mercury	Sr	Strontium
I	Iodine	Ta	Tantalum
In	Indium	Tc	Technetium
Ir	Iridium	Te	Tellurium
K	Potassium	Ti	Titanium
Kr	Krypton	Tl	Thallium
La	Lanthanum	V	Vanadium
Li	Lithium	W	Tungsten
		Xe	Xenon
		Y	Yttrium
		Zn	Zinc
		Zr	Zirconium

Solar System Facts

Planet	Distance From Sun	Revolution (Year)	Rotation (Days)	Diameter	Known Satellites
Mercury	57,900,000 km	88 days	59 days	4,880 km	0
Venus	108,200,000 km	224 days	243 days	12,100 km	0
Earth	149,600,000 km	365 days	24 hours	12,756 km	1
Mars	227,900,000 km	687 days	24 hours	6,794 km	2
Jupiter	778,300,000 km	12 years	10 hours	142,984 km	16
Saturn	1,429,000,000 km	29 years	11 hours	120,536 km	17
Uranus	2,875,000,000 km	84 years	17 hours	51,100 km	15
Neptune	4,504,000,000 km	165 years	18 hours	49,200 km	2
Pluto	5,900,000,000 km	248 years	6 days	3,200 km	1

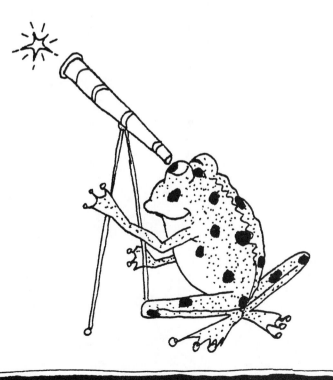